CANADIAN
CONSTITUTIONAL
DILEMMAS
REVISITED

CANADIAN
CONSTITUTIONAL
DILEMMAS
REVISITED

Denis N. Magnusson and Daniel A. Soberman Editors

INSITUTE OF
INTERGOVERNMENTAL
RELATIONS

INSTITUT DES
RELATIONS
INTERGOUVERNEMENTALES

Canadian Cataloguing in Publication Data

Main entry under title:

Canadian constitutional dilemmas revisited

Based on a symposium entitled Continuing Canadian constitutional dilemmas, held in Kingston, Ont., Oct. 1993, in honour of William R. Lederman.
Includes some text in French.
Includes bibliographical references.
ISBN 0-88911-595-8 (bound)   ISBN 0-88911-593-1 (pbk.)

1. Canada – Constitutional law – Congresses. 2. Separation of powers – Canada – Congresses. 3. Canada. Canadian Charter of Rights and Freedoms – Congresses. I. Magnusson, Denis N. II. Soberman, D. A., 1929-   .
III. Lederman, W. R. (William Ralph), 1916-1992. IV. Queen's University (Kingston, Ont.). Institute of Intergovernmental Relations.

JL65.1997.C36 1997   342.71   C97-931449-6

Contents

Preface

This collection of commentaries was produced from a Symposium in honour of the late William R. Lederman held in Kingston, Ontario in October, 1993. The Symposium bore the title *Continuing Canadian Constitutional Dilemmas* after the title of a collection of Bill Lederman's essays published by Butterworth & Co. (Canada) in 1981.

The following collection of commentaries and essays was drawn from the transcript of the main speakers' remarks at the Symposium. The following commentaries should be read, then, as being delivered in October, 1993, and do not generally take account of subsequent events. While the production of this collection a considerable time after the original presentation of these papers, we believe that the collection remains valuable both for its reflection on Bill Lederman's role in Canadian constitutional scholarship, and for the insights of our distinguished contributors on some Canadian constitutional dilemmas, revisited.

The commentaries appear in this collection under six headings in the order in which they were presented at the Symposium.

The program for the original Symposium had invited two participants to address Federalism, "reflecting Bill Lederman's concerns with the distribution of powers" under the Canadian constitution. One of those contributors is included here in Part I, Federalism.

Under Part 2 our two contributors were asked to address Separation of Powers, "reflecting Bill Lederman's concerns with the nature and role of the judicial branch".

In the original Symposium program, Parts 3 to 6 appeared as sessions on different dimensions of the Canadian *Charter of Rights and Freedoms*.

Under Part 3, our two contributors were asked to consider Equality Rights and in Part 4, the contributors addressed Freedom of Expression. Part 5 was focused on Criminal Law under the Charter while Part 6 was dedicated to Group Rights.

Part 7 of this collection represents the contributions of the three main participants in a forum on "Judicial Independence and Responsibility".

This collection concludes with a remembrance of Bill Lederman delivered at the original Symposium dinner by a former student of Bill's at the Queen's Faculty of Law.

Denis Magnusson

DEDICATION

William Ralph Lederman,
O.C., Q.C., B.A., LL.B., B.C.L., LL.D., F.R.S.C.
(1916-1992)

Bill Lederman was a leading constitutional authority and builder of modern legal education in Canada.

Fascinated by foundational concepts, he focused his scholarship on the basic concepts of social order, legalism, common law adjudication, and public government. For him, it was essential that policies and legal arguments be rooted in the basic values and structures of organized society.

Born in Regina, Saskatchewan, Bill Lederman grew up on the Prairies, and received his B.A. and LL.B. from the University of Saskatchewan. After distinguished wartime service, he completed his B.C.L. at Oxford in 1948, having been awarded Rhodes and Vinerian Scholarships. He then returned to Canada and taught in the Faculties of Law at Saskatchewan and Dalhousie before accepting an appointment in 1958 as the first Dean of Law at Queen's University.

In the ten years of his deanship, Bill Lederman brought the student enrolment, the faculty complement, and the Law Library collection up to a size that would support a sophisticated law curriculum. He consistently appointed to the faculty young scholars with an interdisciplinary bent, thus laying the groundwork for a faculty that is diverse, critical, open to new perspectives, and politically aware.

Bill Lederman was a gentle and committed man, as well as a profoundly influential legal academic. He was a beloved dean, a fine teacher, a thoughtful colleague, a kind and steadfast friend.

PARTICIPANTS IN THE CONTINUING CANADIAN CONSTITUTIONAL DILEMMAS SYMPOSIUM OCTOBER, 1993

(In order of appearance of commentaries with institutions and appointments at the time of the original Symposium, October, 1993)

Chevrette, François, Professeur titulaire, Faculté de Droit, Université de Montréal

Monahan, Patrick, Professor, Osgoode Hall Law School, York University.

Elliot, Robin, Professor, Faculty of Law, University of British Columbia

Jackman, Martha, Associate Professor, Faculty of Law, Common Law Section, University of Ottawa

Majury, Diana, Associate Professor, Department of Law, Carleton University

Smith, C. Lynn, Professor and Dean, Faculty of Law, University of British Columbia

MacKay, Wayne, Professor, Faculty of Law, Dalhousie University

Mahoney, Kathleen, Professor, Faculty of Law, University of Calgary

Boyle, Christine, Professor, Faculty of Law, University of British Columbia

Stuart, Donald, Professor, Faculty of Law, Queen's University

Frémont, Jacques, Professeur agrégé, Faculté de Droit, Université de Montréal

Johnston, Darlene, Assistant Professor, Faculty of Law, Common Law Section, University of Ottawa

Scott, Ian, Barrister and Solicitor, Gowling, Strathy, Henderson, Toronto

Wilson, Bertha, Justice of the Supreme Court of Canada (ret.)

Cromwell, Tom, Professor, Faculty of Law, Dalhousie University

Thomson, George, Deputy Attorney-General, Ontario

PART ONE

FEDERALISM

Lederman's Place in Federalism Scholarship

Patrick Monahan

I am very pleased to have been invited to participate in this symposium in honour of Bill Lederman. Although I did not know Bill well, I did have occasion to meet him in the early 1980's when I was just beginning my career as a Law teacher. I had been told by one of my senior colleagues at Osgoode Hall, who will remain nameless, that while it was absolutely essential that we law professors spend our time diligently writing law review articles few people read the finished product. I was told that there had been studies done on this issue. While my colleague didn't cite the studies, he assured me that they indicated that a Law Review article in Canada was read by an average of 3.1 persons. He continued, it was none the less absolutely essential that we spend our time writing these articles for these lonely readers and making our little contributions to scholarship. I said "thats fine" and went about my business. I tried to write a few things because there is the minor matter of getting tenure.

Shortly after I had published my very first article, I happened to attend a conference where Professor Lederman was speaking. I took the liberty of introducing myself to him. "Professor Lederman, my name is Patrick Monahan" I said. "Oh", he said, "yes, I read this article that you've written".

I was absolutely stunned. Here was one of the mythical 3.1 persons! And not just anybody. Here was Bill Lederman who was, in my estimation, one of the two leading English Canadian constitutional scholars of the day, saying he had read my little article. He demonstrated that he had actually read the thing by making some comments, which I recall seemed somewhat positive. I was absolutely taken aback. I thought, "well, maybe these articles are worth something after all." Here is someone with the rank and the reputation of Bill Lederman who was actually taking the time to read the work of a beginning scholar. I wondered whether my senior colleague at Osgoode had been unduly pessimistic about the significance of our work.

In later years, I heard similar stories from others about Bill Lederman's special interest in beginning scholars. Like me, many others have been touched and encouraged by his kindness and his attitude towards young scholars. Jim MacPherson, for example, the former Dean at Osgoode who has just recently been appointed to the Bench, told me a similar story of an incident that took place in the late 70's when he had just begun teaching at the University of Victoria. Lederman seemed qenuinely interested in the ideas of young scholars. He took the time to suggest where he thought they might be saying something worthwhile, but also where they might perhaps be straying a little bit off track. Bill Lederman seemed to see himself in some sense as having a responsibility to bring young scholars along and to encourage them in their scholarship. That was in a very personal way very important to me and to many others.

It was some years later, in the late 1980's, that I was struck once again by Professor Lederman's sense of responsibility to the larger community. It was immediately following the negotiation of the Meech Lake Accord in 1987. I recall very distinctly the moment when Professor Lederman testified before the Parliamentary committee, which held its hearing in the summer of 1987. I was fortunate enough to have been able to play a very small role in advising some of the decision makers in the process. Those of us who had been involved as advisers were very interested to know what Bill Lederman thought about the Meech Lake Accord. We regarded Bill Lederman as a very special academic. In academia the siren call of principle is very strong. The siren call of principle suggests that things are either right or they are wrong. Sittingin the university it is easy to say, "well I have a set of abstract principles that I know to be right. I want to measure the work of politicians and the work of legislatures against this set of abstract principles." Of course, if the work of the politicians doesn't precisely match up with the principles (as it rarely does) then the politicians must be wrong.

But Bill Lederman did not subscribe to that approach, Bill Lederman was certainly a very principled person and a very principled academic. But he also understood the need for compromise. His writings reflected the fact that the practical realities of federalism in a country such as Canada could never accord with a set of abstract principles. So it was of particular interest for us to hear what Professor Lederman would have to say about the Meech Lake Accord. I remember watching along with my colleagues on the television as he appeared and gave his testimony. As you may recall, he spoke very strongly in favour of the Accord. I must tell you that was important to me and others. There was a vigorous debate on the Accord, with strong arguments put forth on both sides. It was important for those of us who had participated to know that someone of the stature, independence and quality of Bill Lederman would find the Accord to be acceptable. I know there are people in this room who took a different view and continue to do so. I simply offer that from my own personal perspective, Bill Lederman's support for Meech Lake confirmed his stature in my eyes as an academic with the special ability to bridge the gap between the world of the academy and the world of practical constitutional politics.

This symposium is important because it provides an opportunity to situate Bill Lederman in the history of constitutional scholarship in Canada. I would venture the observation that Bill Lederman's contribution has been somewhat underrated in English Canada. In my view, Bill Lederman stands at the very pinnacle of English Canadian constitutional scholarship. He stands in a select class with just two others. These three eminent constitutional scholars have shaped English Canadian constitutional thinking over the past 60 years.

Who are the other two, who along with Bill Lederman, occupy this lofty status? The first is, of course, Bora Laskin, Bill Lederman's contemporary and a towering presence in Canadian constitutional thought. I'll have more to say about Professor Lederman and Chief Justice Laskin in a moment. The final member of this select category is my colleague and friend at Osgoode, Peter Hogg. Peter Hogg's book *Constitutional Law of Canada* has already become a kind of *Blackstone's Commentaries* of Canadian constitutional law. It has become a staple in every Canadian lawyer's library. It is now required reading, not only for lawyers, but for all judges, and particularly judges on the Supreme Court of Canada. On more than one occasion in recent years, Professor Hogg he has been referred to a the "10th Justice" on the Supreme Court. His work has been cited more frequently by the Court than that of any other scholar. I regard Peter Hogg as falling in the same category as Laskin and Lederman.

I want to focus my remarks today on the respective contributions made by Bill Lederman and Bora Laskin. I think the best way to appreciate Bill Lederman's contribution is by comparing and contrasting his work with that of his contemporary, Bora Laskin. In a sense, the evolution of constitutional thinking in English Canada and, indeed, in Canada as a whole over the last 50 years, is the story of the interplay and the exchange of ideas between these two thoughtful Canadians.

Bora Laskin exemplified the centralist vision of Canadian Federalism. He believed passionately in the need for a strong central government. The lifelong project of Bora Laskin, as we all know, was to significantly strengthen the powers of the central Government, and to break with the constitutional traditions of the Privy Council. Bill Lederman was the opposite side of that same coin. The Lederman tradition is the tradition of classical federalism. It is a traditionthat emphasized the need for continuity with the work of the Privy Council. In tracing the clash of ideas between Laskin and Lederman, both at the intellectual level and the practical level, we see the unfolding shape of the living constitution in this country.

Let me just take a few moments to refer to Bora Laskin because it is only through understanding Laskin's project I think that we can appreciate the significance of Bill Lederman's role and contribution. The Laskin project was a project that arose out of the depression and the Second World War. Through that experience, English Canada came to believe very strongly in the need to strengthen the powers of the central Government. The existing powers of the Central Government seemed to be inadequate to meet the challenges posed by the depression. The experience of the war years, where powers had been centralized in Ottawa, seemed to offer to people such as Laskin, Frank Scott, and otherst the vision of a new kind of federalism. Laskin and Scott were unrelenting in their critique of the Privy Council. Their critique focused, to a very large measure, on the interpretation that the Privy Council had given to the general power, the "peace, order and good government power", in s.91 of the *Constitution Act*. The theory of Laskin and others was that this power had been wrongly interpreted by the Privy Council. It had been wrongly interpreted because, according to Laskin, it was not simply a residual power sitting at the end of the line after you had looked at the list of exclusive federal and provincial powers. Rather, it should be interpreted as a overarching power, giving the Federal Parliament the authority to enact laws that are necessary in the national interest. It was said that the Privy Council had mistakenly focused on the lists of enumerated powers in s.91 and s.92 and forgotten the peace order and good government power. Laskin urged for a resuscitation of the general power. He believed that if this were done, the Federal Parliament would possess the powers that were needed in order to deal with Canada's place and challenge in the world in the 20th century.

Now the Lederman view was different. It was a view that proceeded from a classical federalist vision. I was interested to learn, in conversation with Bill's son Lewis Lederman, that Bill was not always of that view. In fact Lewis tells me that in the late 40's and early 50's his father's views were "of the Bora Laskin school". He subscribed to the view that what was needed was a strong central government. But in his writings through the 50's and on into the early 60's we began to see a different Lederman emerge. Lederman began developing a theory that he identified as a kind of "moderate pragmatism". He sought to achieve a balance between the Federal and Provincial Governments, a balance that essentially preserved and built upon the core of the work of the Privy Council. For Lederman, the focus of a division of powers analysis should remain with the lists of enumerated powers in section 91 and 92. He rejected the Laskin view to the effect that the courts should revisit their approach to the division of powers and place much greater weight on the Peace Order and Good Government ("POGG") power of s. 91 of the *B.N.A. Act.*

The best statement of the Lederman philosophy in relation to the division of powers is his article "Unity and Diversity in Canadian Federalism" published in the *Canadian Bar Review* in 1975.[1] Not only does this article represent the best statement of Lederman's views on the division of power, it seems to me to be, if not the best, one of the very best articles that has ever been written on the division of powers in Canada. The article was originally a public lecture delivered in June of 1975, and was published in the *Bar Review* in December of that year. Lederman put forward a vision of Canadian Federalism that was founded on three principles. First, was the principle of balance. According to this first principle, there needs to be a balance or an equilibrium between the powers of the federal Parliament and those of the provincial legislatures. What this means in practice, according to Lederman, is that in interpreting the various powers in s.91 and in s.92 we must interpret them so as to insure that neither set of powers or categories will over-whelm the other. Each specific head of power should be interpreted in a manner that is self-limiting. This will ensure some rough balance between the respective powers of the Parliament of Canada and the provincial legislatures. That was the first principle.

The second principle was that of incrementalism or gradualism. This principle emphasized the need for continuity, the need to take small steps rather than large steps. Lederman believed in building on our experience and our traditions, rather than breaking with the past. This was a way of avoiding large mistakes.

The third Lederman principle is one of pragmatism or, as François Chevrette described it, 'functionalism'. Lederman understood that in interpreting the Con-stitution we are not engaging in a purely logical or textual analysis. The courts are policymakers who ultimately have to consider the results of their decisions. What will it mean *in practice* to interpret the Constitution in this way as opposed to that way? This was the question Lederman urged upon courts and lawyers. Taken together, these three principles, which he described as a kind of moderate prag-matism, inform his whole approach to the division of powers.

His *Bar Review* article did not deal just with matters of high theory. He also put forward a specific interpretation of the 'POGG' power in s.91 of the *BNA Act*. The Lederman interpretation was a response to the project of Bora Laskin and others who, since 1945 had been arguing for the need to expand this power. And what Lederman advanced was an idea which was at the time quite novel. He began by saying, "well I recognize that there is a need to provide some additional room or scope for the powers of the federal Parliament". In other words he did not dismiss out of hand the argument that there needed to be some adjustment in federal power. He said, in developing this power we must ensure that it does not overwhelm or nullify the powers of the provinces. He proceeded to offer some criteria to achieve that result. He essentially said that we should only recognize the use of the Peace Order and Good Government power in relation to matters that have a unity and distinctiveness. This internal unity sets these matters apart from other matters so that, in recognizing them as falling under federal authority, we do not upset the balance that exists in our Constitution between federal and provincial powers. The fact that this new matter has a distinctiveness and unity means that it can be confined and it will not overwhelm provincial powers. It is not all encompassing. This analysis is consistent as well with the second principle of continuity, or incrementalism, which says that we should not have radical breaks with the past. His analysis was also a functional analysis because he related his theory to the practical outcomes it would produce. He considered the case of aviation. In practical terms, he said it is not functional to divide authority over aviation between Canada and the provinces because airplanes and air space know no provincial boundaries. So it makes sense in functional terms to give aviation to the federal government. Aviation has this unity, this distinctiveness, and recognizing it as a matter under federal authority will not interfere with provincial powers.

He offered some other more general comments that are of particular contemporary relevance. He observed that very general categories, like "culture" or "pollution" are not fit to be recognised as categories for purposes of s.91 and 92 of in the Constitution Act. It's interesting tospeculate as to what he would have said about the Charlottetown Accord. One of Charlottetown's provisions would have recognized "culture" as a head of exclusive provincial jurisdiction. While we don't know for certain what he would have thought about that, we have a pretty good idea based on his 1975 article.

Well, circumstances were to conspire to make this article play a very important role in the development of our constitutional law. In the months after he had delivered his lecture the Government of Canada announced its anti-inflation program in October of that year. There was obviously great controversy about the program and in March 1976 the federal government referred to a series of questions to the Supreme Court of Canada asking about Parliament's authority to enact the Anti-inflation Act. Bora Laskin was the Chief Justice of Canada at that time. The federal government put forward an argument that seemed designed to appeal to Laskin's view of the POGG power. The Government of Canada argued that inflation is a matter of serious national concern. It is a very important matter and the only way to deal with it is through this legislation. Therefore, Canada said, the legislation can be supported through the federal general power.

The case came before the Supreme Court of Canada in June of 1976. It so happened that Bill Lederman had been retained to argue the case on behalf of the Renfrew County Teachers Association. I am told, by his son Lew, it was the first and only time that he ever appeared in court. I was not there when the case was argued but I'm told by others who were that it was a very dramatic moment. In those days the Supreme Court of Canada would take a week to hear an important case, rather than half a day the way they do now. The custom is to permit two counsel for each of the parties to address the court. Well I am told that before the commencement of the argument, Mr. Aubrey Golden who was the lead counsel for the Renfrew County Teachers, stood up to make a special request. Mr. Golden acknowledged that the custom was to have only two counsel address the Court in oral argument. Mr. Golden sought leave for special exception to be made in this case. "I have my junior counsel seated immediately to my right, Mr. Paul Cavalluzzo who will argue part of the case for our client", he said. I should note here that Mr. Cavalluzzo has gone on to become a very renowned counsel in this province and in the country. Mr Golden continued "but seated to Mr. Cavalluzzo's right is Professor Bill Lederman. I would like very much to have the benefit of Professor Lederman's argument as well. So I beg leave to have Professor Lederman argue in addition to myself and Mr. Cavalluzzo which would mean we would have three counsel address the court". "Well Mr. Golden", the Chief Justice said, "I'm sorry, but there is absolutely no way that we can violate our rules. We can only allow two counsel per party, which means that we simply can't accommodate Professor Lederman."

Mr. Golden sat down and I guess thought about this for a while. When it came time then for him to present his argument he stood up and said, "Well my Lord, I fully accept the fact that I can only have two counsel but I have decided to change the order. I'm now going to move Professor Lederman to the number two spot. I will argue first and Professor Lederman will speak second." Well there was really nothing the Chief Justice could do about that because certainly Mr. Golden was well within his rights to have two counsel address the court. Eventually it came time for Professor Lederman to make his argument. Of course, he advanced to the court precisely the argument that he had developed in his Bar Review article. I am told by those who were there that day that it was a very important and almost an electric moment. After spending their careers developing quite different visions of the constitution, here was the moment where these two great thinkers would finally confront each other. And what better setting for this historic clash of ideas than the main courtroom of the Supreme Court of Canada.

We all know the power of the intellect of Bora Laskin. Some may also know of his willingness to advance his ideas in shall we say a forceful and forthright manner. I am told that he did so on that occasion. But Bill Lederman in his gentlemanly way put forward his arguments and made his case to the full court. And when it came time for nine judges of the Court to render their judgment it became apparent that the federal government had failed to achieve the breakthrough it had been hoping for. While the federal government won the case, the court had to fall back on the theory of an "emergency" in order to uphold the legislation. It was only on the basis that inflation was an emergency that this legislation could be justified. Moreover Mr. Justice Beetz along with the other Quebec judges took up the argument that Professor Lederman had advanced in his Bar Review article. Mr. Justice Beetz made specific reference to the Lederman view and advanced it as the basis of the operation of the federal general power. Mr. Justice Beetz argued that the general power was only available in relation to discrete, limited areas. "Inflation" was too broad a subject to fit within POGG.

Now Mr. Justice Beetz at that time was not able to attract a majority of the Court to his view. In the years since the *Anti-inflation* case was decided, the Lederman/Beetz view has become the established wisdom in the interpretation of the federal general power. Consider the *Crown Zellerbach*[2] case decided a couple of years ago by the Supreme Court of Canada by a 4 to 3 margin. While there was a very sharp division of opinion in that case in terms of the result, all of the Judges operated within the framework of the Lederman/Beetz view of the federal general power. What they disagreed about was how this framework applied in this particular case, but all of them accepted that was the framework to apply. So it turns out that it was the Lederman view that eventually emerged as the established conventional wisdom in relation to the federal general power.

I wanted to deal briefly with one other area in relation to Lederman's influence on the evolution of the division of powers. This is an area where Bill Lederman's contribution has been insufficiently appreciated. I refer to the area of constitutional amendment. One of Bill Lederman's particular concerns was how the constitution can and should be amended. His writing emphasizes a respect for tradition, constitutional convention, and also a need to balance federal and provincial powers. This was evident in 1978 when the federal government introduced Bill C-60, proposing a very comprehensive amendment to the Constitution, in particular, an amendment to the Senate. The federal government proposed to recast the Senate as a "House of the Provinces" with the Senators appointed by the Premiers. The majority of commentators at that time said that this change to the Senate could be accomplished by the federal Parliament acting alone by virtue of its power under s.91.1 of the Constitution Act of 1867. Section 91.1 was the power to amend "the Constitution of Canada", which was added to the list of federal powers in 1949. The majority view, amongst commentators at that time, was that this 91.1 power gave the Parliament of Canada unilateral authority to enact that change.

Bill Lederman was a dissenter in English Canada on that issue. In fact he appeared in front of the Parliamentary Committee holding hearings on the bill and said, "I'm sorry I don't think you have the power to do this". The power to change the Senate implicates fundamental provincial interests and therefore cannot be accomplished by the Parliament of Canada acting alone. Such an amendment requires legislation enacted by Westminster.

I was at that time a student at Osgoode Hall Law School. In fact Professor Hogg was teaching me Constitutional law. Professor Hogg also went up to Ottawa to testify before the Parliamentary Committee. I remember him saying he was very concerned because, although he had testified that Bill C-60 was constitutional, Professor Lederman had taken the opposite view. Professor Hogg explained to his students that he always disagreed with Professor Lederman at his peril, because Lederman almost always turned out to be right. So although he still thought that the Parliament of Canada could do this on its own, he had noted with apprehension the difference of opinion with Bill Lederman. Of course, it turns out that it was Professor Lederman who was right. In 1979, the Supreme Court of Canada, by a vote of 9 to 0, agreed with the Lederman view. All those commentators who thought that the Parliament of Canada could unilaterally change the Senate had turned out to be wrong.

This led very soon after to the "patriation round" of constitutional amendment which began in October 1980. On October 2, the Federal Government tabled a constitutional resolution asking the British Parliament to patriate the Constitution, and to enact a new amending formula and a Charter of Rights. Once again the Government of Canada took the position that it had the power to do this unilaterally. It didn't need any provincial consent, despite the fact that the amendment directly affected provincial powers. Well it was perhaps not very surprising that the Supreme Court of Canada attempted to strike a compromise and a very interesting one at that. The Supreme Court of Canada determined that there was a constitutional convention requiring provincial consent to the resolution. What was unexpected was the Court's ruling that "substantial consent" and not unaminous consent, was required. Now many commentators said, where is the Court getting this idea of "substantial consent"? How many provinces adds up to "substantial", is it 7, is it 8, is it 9?

Interestingly enough, Professor Lederman back in 1978 had originally put forward precisely this argument about substantial consent. In an article published in the Law Society Lectures in 1978[3] Professor Lederman emphasized that our constitutional position must evolve to take into account changing circumstances. While some provincial consent is necessary for important amendments it would not be appropriate for a province such as Prince Edward Island to block a constitutional amendment that was supported by the Government of Canada and the other nine provinces. In his view, it would be in accord with fundamental values in Canada to say, that as long as you have at least "substantial consent" of the provinces, an amendment could proceed to Westminster.

Lederman's 1978 article was cited by the Supreme Court of Canada in the *Patriation Reference*. Although it is not referred to in the judgment of the majority written by Mr. Justice Beetz on the issue of constitutional convention, it was cited by Chief Justice Bora Laskin in dissent. How could anyone say that Prince Edward Island's consent was not required but Ontario's and Quebec's were, Laskin asked. There is absolutely no basis in law for this theory other than a majority of the Supreme Court of Canada happened to agree with it. Why? They saw in it the germ of a compromise and the foundation for accommodation. The Lederman formula, while perhaps 'unprincipled' and amorphous, offers a practical resolution of a dispute that people can live with. Once again, the Lederman values of compromise, continuity and balancefound favour with the Supreme Court of Canada.

Let me make very brief reference to one other article by Bill Lederman on the division of powers. As I was preparing for this talk I re-read the essays in his book *Continuing Canadian Constitutional Dilemmas* and I came across an article he had written on the Treaty Power.[4] I was particularly interested in that essay because, as you may know, the Ontario Government has recently announced it wishes to challenge the implementation of the North American Free Trade Agreement by the Parliament of Canada. I thought, what did Bill Lederman have to say about this? He puts forward a very interesting and original theory. The leading case in this area is the 1937 *Labour Conventions* case which says that treaties dealing with matters under provincial jurisdiction must be implemented by the provinces. You might have expected that Lederman, as a defender of the Privy Council, would have supported the Labour Conventions case, but he doesn't. Labour Conventions, he says, is too restrictive of federal authority. There should be greater scope for the federal Parliament to implement treaty obligations. On the other hand, he says, we don't want to give the federal Parliament *carte blanche* to implement any and all treaties that it may sign. So he proposes a middle ground. He argues that the federal Parliament should have the power to implement treaties *except* in cases where they affect "fundamental" provincial interests.

Now my immediate reaction, upon reading this, was to say, well that doesn't sound very plausible. How are we supposed to distinguish between those provincial interests that are fundamental and those that are not? Just like Chief Justice Bora Laskin asked in 1981, how are we supposed to make sense of a requirement like "substantial" provincial consent? If I were a betting man I wouldn't want to wager a large sum against Bill Lederman and his instincts as to where a court would come out on this issue. It seems that the courts may soon be asked to decide that very issue.

I want to close by referring again to Lederman's 1978 essay "Constitutional Amendment and Canadian Unity". This essay is worth re-reading by concerned

Canadians in the months and years ahead. I expect that next week's federal election will give us a different kind of Parliament than we have ever had before. In responding to that new situation we should be mindful of Bill Lederman's words back in 1978, which was also a time of uncertainty for this country. Lederman spoke not only of the need to find an accommodation between English-speaking and French- speaking Canadians for our own domestic reasons, but also in terms of Canada's role in the world community. Canada provides the world with an example of how major linguistic and ethnic groups can live together, under a federal constitution, and maintain both unity and diversity in proper measure. He concludes his essay with these words, "Of course we must concern ourselves with what French-speaking Canadians have a right to expect and with what English-speaking Canadians have a right to expect". "But", he says, "there is an overriding question: what does the rest of the world have a right to expect from Canada?" That perspective which focuses on Canada's place in the world community is an important one that is too often ignored. It is a world view that would benefit all Canadians as we continue to grapple with the dilemmas and constitutional conundrums which no doubt will occupy us for many years yet to come.

NOTES

1. "Unity and Diversity in Canadian Federalism: Ideals and Methods of Moderation", (1975), 53 *Canadian Bar Review* 597.
2. *R. v. Crown Zellerbach Canada Ltd.*, [1988] 1 S.C.R. 401.
3. "Constitutional Amendment and Canadian Unity", *Special Lectures of the Law Society of Upper Canada 1978: The Constitution and the Future of Canada* (Toronto: Richard De Boo Ltd., 1978).
4 . "Legislative Power to Implement Treaty Obligations in Canada", in *Continuing Canadian Constitutional Dilemmas: Essays on the Constitutional History, Public Law and Federal System of Canada* (Toronto: Butterworths, 1981.)

PART TWO

SEPARATION OF POWERS

Rethinking Section 96: From a Question of Power to a Question of Rights

Robin Elliot

Let me begin by paying tribute to Professor Lederman, in whose honour this symposium has been organized. I have a clear recollection of relying very heavily on Professor Lederman's work, particularly in the division of powers area, when I started teaching constitutional law back in the mid-1970's. In fact, the casebook that I then used was the first edition of what became known as Whyte and Lederman. I seldom had recourse to Professor Lederman's writings for the purpose of finding out what the law was; what made those writings so valuable to me as a young teacher was Professor Lederman's ability to identify the foundational issues in the field of Canadian constitutional law and to provide, as we have heard already this morning, the conceptual frameworks within which we could deal with those issues in a systematic and comprehensive manner. What was particularly appealing to me about those frameworks was that they were grounded in, and gave explicit voice to, the values that Professor Lederman believed to lie at the foundation of our particular system of government. Moreover, he was prepared to discuss those values — the rule of law, judicial independence, community, and liberty — at some length. Now that we have the *Charter of Rights and Freedoms* it is expected that those who write in the field of constitutional law will engage these values directly. Such was not the case in the pre-*Charter* era in which Professor Lederman wrote most of his scholarship. His willingness to approach constitutional law scholarship in this way represented a break with tradition, and like all such breaks, no doubt took some courage on his part. Be that as it may, it greatly enhanced the value of the contribution that he made to the field and to all of us. Perhaps especially young scholars entering the field owe him a considerable debt of gratitude.

Important as it is on occasions such as this to remember and mark Professor Lederman's contribution to our understanding of Canadian constitutional law, I think it important also to say something about him as a human being. I did not know Professor Lederman well, but we did cross paths on several occasions and I could not help but be impressed by his personal warmth, kindness and the genuine interest that he showed in the work of younger scholars like myself. One quality that stood out above all the others, at least to me, was his humility. I will never forget a chance meeting that took place in the halls of the Faculty of Law at the University of British Columbia in the mid-1980's, shortly after Professor Lederman had published a typically thoughtful and thought provoking piece on the *Charter of Rights and Freedoms*. He asked me if I had read the piece and when I answered "Yes, I most certainly have", he went on to ask me for my reaction to it. It was clear both from the way in which he formulated the question and the tone in which he asked it that he was genuinely concerned that the piece might be found wanting in some way. My initial reaction to the question was to be astounded that someone of his stature would not only doubt the quality of his work but confess to such doubts openly and to a much younger colleague. That quickly turned into a sense of admiration for the kind of person who was capable of such humility, the kind of person that Professor Lederman obviously was. Incidentally, I assured him that the piece lived up to the high standards that he had set for himself in his earlier work in the field of constitutional law and we went on to have a very stimulating, if unfortunately brief, discussion about some of the views he had expressed in the piece.

The topic that I have been asked to speak to this morning is, like the division of powers between Parliament and the provincial legislatures, a feature of Canada's constitution that was of great interest to Professor Lederman and in which he was a strong believer — the mini separation of powers doctrine fashioned by the Privy Council out of the judicature provisions of the *Constitution Act, 1867*, particularly section 96. My approach to this topic will differ somewhat from the approaches that Professors Chevrette and Monahan took to their topics earlier this morning, in that I will spend less time talking about the influence that Professor Lederman had in this area than I will about the area itself. The reason for this difference lies in the nature of the request that John Whyte made to me when he asked me to participate in this symposium several months ago. His suggestion was that I should provide an overview of recent developments in the area along with some critical perspective thereon.

What follows can be divided into four parts. As there may be people in the audience who are not familiar with this rather obscure area of Canadian constitutional law, I am going to begin with something of a primer on the doctrine surrounding section 96. I will then note some of the more significant developments

in this area in the last decade or so; the focus here will be on doctrinal developments but reference will also be made to a constitutional amendment proposal
bearing on this area. Next, I want to provide an abbreviated critique of the existing doctrine and more fundamentally of the approach to the judicature provisions
out of which this doctrine has evolved. I will conclude by suggesting a new way
of thinking about this area, one that bears no small resemblance to the approach
taken to it by Professor Lederman in his classic piece on the independence of the
judiciary.[1]

I begin with the primer. Although we in Canada have no separation of powers
doctrine of the kind that Americans can claim, our courts — first the Privy Council and then the Supreme Court of Canada — have fashioned a body of constitutional doctrine that bears at least a limited resemblance to such a doctrine.[2] That
body of doctrine has been constructed on the basis of the apparently innocuous
provision with which the judicature part of the *Constitution Act, 1867* begins,
section 96:

> The Governor General shall appoint the Judges of the Superior, District and County
> Courts in each Province, except those of the Court of Probate in Nova Scotia and
> New Brunswick.

At the heart of the doctrine is a functional interpretation of the phrase "Judges of
the Superior, District, and County Courts in each Province". Those words have
been interpreted to mean, in effect, "persons who perform the functions of judges
of the Superior, District, and County Courts in each Province". According to this
interpretation, all such persons must as a matter of constitutional law be appointed
by the Governor General (in other words, by the federal order of government).
Hence, any person appointed by a *provincial* government who performs the function of a section 96 court judge is acting unconstitutionally or, putting it somewhat differently, has been appointed illegally. By virtue of this functional interpretation of section 96, numerous challenges have been brought over the years to
a broad range of statutory provisions allocating to provincially appointed officials adjudicative functions of various types. Some of these challenges have been
directed against provincial court judges, others against the members of provincially established administrative tribunals. The majority of these challenges have
failed, but enough have succeeded for the doctrine to be something of a thorn in
the side of reform-minded governments.

The critical question in the application of the doctrine, of course, is how one
decides whether or not a particular person is performing the functions of a section
96 court judge. That question is generally understood to have been resolved by
the decision in 1981 of the Supreme Court of Canada in *Reference re Residential
Tenancies Act*,[3] a case out of the province of Ontario involving the power of

provincially appointed members of an administrative tribunal to adjudicate certain kinds of landlord and tenant disputes. Chief Justice Dickson, writing for the Court in that case, and purporting to summarize what he understood to have been the doctrine developed in earlier cases, set out a three-part test for determining whether or not a particular adjudicative function is appropriately characterized as a section 96 court function and hence a function that can be constitutionally performed only by federal appointees.[4] The first part of the test, which takes the form of an historical inquiry, asks whether or not the adjudicative function in question "broadly conforms" to a function performed by section 96 court judges at the time of Confederation. If that question is answered in the negative, the function will not be characterized as a section 96 court function and there is no constitutional bar to its being allocated to a provincial appointee. However, if the answer to the question is in the affirmative, one proceeds to the next step in the test which asks whether or not, viewed in isolation, the function can be said to be a "judicial" function. According to Chief Justice Dickson, a function will be characterized as "judicial" if it involves the adjudication of a private dispute between parties on the basis of a recognized body of rules and in a manner consistent with fairness and impartiality. If the answer to this second question is in the negative, the function is held not to be a section 96 court function and the challenge to the legislation assigning it to a provincial appointee will be dismissed. If the answer is in the affirmative, one proceeds to the last step in the test, which asks whether or not, viewed in its broader institutional setting, the function remains a "judicial" function or has become something else. According to Chief Justice Dickson, if the function can be said to be the sole or central function of the tribunal in question, the function will continue to be seen as "judicial" and held to be a section 96 court function performable only by persons appointed by the federal government. If, by contrast, the adjudicative function is seen to be ancillary or necessarily incidental to the implementation of broader administrative or policy goals embodied in the enabling statute, the function will no longer be seen to be "judicial" and the challenge to the legislation assigning it to provincial appointees will be dismissed.

It is important, I think, to say a word or two at this juncture about the rationale for erecting this mini separation of powers doctrine out of section 96. Unfortunately, neither the Privy Council nor the Supreme Court of Canada has been particularly forthcoming on this aspect of the matter. Their energies have been devoted far more to fashioning the doctrine itself than to providing a justification for it. Such attempts as have been made to provide a justification have tended to focus on the peculiar character of Canadian federalism in the area of the court system. A good example of this rationale for the doctrine is provided by Justice La Forest's recent judgment in *Scowby v. Glendinning*:

Though legislative powers were divided between two levels of government, a unitary judicial system was established to deal with laws enacted at both levels. Each level of government, therefore, has an interest in the administration of judicial affairs, an interest reflected in constitutional arrangements whereby the provinces were given power to legislate respecting the 'Constitution, Maintenance, and Organization of Provincial Courts', and the federal governmentpower to appoint the judges of the superior, district and county courts. Evidently, if the provinces were completely free to vest the powers of those courts in tribunals of their own making, s. 96 could become a dead letter, and the constitutional scheme contemplated by the Fathers destroyed.[5]

Let me turn now to an overview of recent developments in this area. Two of the developments that I am going to discuss relate to the evolution of mini separation of powers doctrine in the courts, the other to a failed proposal for a constitutional amendment. The first doctrinal development worth noting is the extension of the doctrine to the federal order of government. In 1983, in what has become known as the *McEvoy*[6] case, the Supreme Court of Canada held that section 96 operated as a limit not only on the power of provincial legislatures to assign particular kinds of adjudicative functions to provincial appointees, but as a limit on the power of Parliament to do so also. In so holding, the Court broke with the long standing view, reflected in a number of earlier judicial pronouncements and shared by some academics (but not, I should note, Professor Lederman), that section 96 operated to constrain provincial legislatures only.

The precise nature and scope of the limit on federal power was left open by the judgment in *McEvoy*. The Court there was dealing with what amounted to a wholesale transfer by Parliament of criminal jurisdiction to a proposed new unified criminal court in the province of New Brunswick, the judges of which would be appointed by the government of that province. In the course of holding that federal legislation designed to effect such a transfer would offend section 96, the Court acknowledged that provincial court judges across the country had, over the previous 115 odd years, been the recipients of a good deal of new criminal jurisdiction, and it was evidently reluctant to declare unconstitutional any of the federal legislation by which such transfers had been effected. In effect, the Court drew a distinction between piecemeal transfers of jurisdiction on the one hand and wholesale transfers on the other, with only the latter apparently falling afoul of section 96. (It is interesting to note that in some of the subsequent litigation that has been generated by the decision in *McEvoy*, the lower courts have relied upon this distinction in rejecting challenges to piecemeal transfers of criminal jurisdiction to provincial court judges.[7]) The Supreme Court of Canada has had occasion itself to address the question of whether or not the three part test from *Residential Tenancies* is equally applicable to Parliament, but has yet to resolve that question. Some of the judges appear to hold the view that it is, others that it is not.[8]

That leads me into a discussion of the evolution of the *Residential Tenancies* test in the context of challenges to provincial legislation. Here one can discern two distinct and, in fact, conflicting trends. On the one hand, one finds Justice Wilson in her judgments applying the test faithfully in those cases in which its application is relatively straightforward and refining the test in those cases it is not. On the other hand, one finds Justice La Forest seeking to free himself of the constraints imposed upon him by the test and Justice Wilson's refinements of it. These conflicting tendencies (which are manifested elsewhere and in my view reflect a fundamental difference ofopinion between these two judges about the proper role of formal legal doctrine in constitutional cases) are exemplified by their respective judgments in a case I will call the *Sobeys* case, that the Supreme Court of Canada decided in the late 1980's.[9]

At issue in that case was the validity of provincial legislation assigning to a provincial tribunal jurisdiction to resolve certain kinds of disputes relating to individual employment contracts. In the course of applying the historical part of the *Residential Tenancies* test, Justice Wilson noted that the Court had yet to make it clear which territorial jurisdictions should be examined for the purpose of deciding whether or not the adjudicative function in question "broadly conforms" to those performed by section 96 courts at the time of Confederation. Her answer to that question was that one should look at the situation as it existed in the four founding provinces in the year 1867. In this particular case, however, that examination resulted in a finding that the adjudicative function in question did broadly conform to functions performed at that time by Superior Court judges in two of the provinces but not in the other two. She resolved this dilemma by holding that, in such circumstances, one had to look at the situation in the United Kingdom in 1867. Justice La Forest, who agreed with the result arrived at by Justice Wilson in this case, preferred to write a brief separate concurring judgment in which he disassociated himself from the refinements that she had made to the historical part of the test. In his view, it was unwise for the Court to constrain its freedom of movement in this area in the manner in which her refinements to the test would do. As he put it:

> I would be concerned with an approach that attempted to devise a test with a level of exactness that cannot realistically be applied given the sometimes fragmentary evidence available and the difficulty of weighing its relevance in a modern setting. What requires determination is whether the jurisdiction of a judicial institution is in broad conformity with that of a s. 96 court as these institutions were understood at Confederation. In doing this, I think we should avoid too much precision in a matter that is inevitably imprecise, as well as mechanistic tests for determining the precise

measure of evidence required. What we must do is exercise the best judgment we can in the light of the information before us and what we know to be the functions and purposes of s. 96 courts.[10]

In opting for a less formalistic approach in this area, Justice La Forest can be said to be following in the footsteps of former Chief Justice Laskin. The author of a number of important section 96 decisions while he served on the Supreme Court, he made no attempt to prescribe a comprehensive and rigorous test or set of rules for such cases, preferring instead to deal with each case on its own on the basis of considerations he thought to be relevant to it. A good example of this preference is his judgment for the Court in the *Crevier*[11] case, in which he held that a privative clause purporting to preclude judicial review of decisions relating to the jurisdiction of provincial administrative tribunals violated s. 96. Even though that case was decided a matter of a few months after *Residential Tenancies*, he made no reference to the test set forth in that case and, in fact, virtually ignored it completely.

However, in spite of first Chief Justice Laskin's and now Justice La Forest's attempts to relax the hold of the *Residential Tenancies* test, that test has never been formally rejected, and it appears to remain the preferred approach of a majority of the judges now on the Court. In *Sobeys*, for example, Wilson J. was writing for four of the seven judges that sat on that case, LaForest J. for only three. One has to assume, therefore, that this is the test that is going to be applied in most if not all section 96 cases today.

The last development to which I wish to make reference is the proposal made by the federal government back in 1983 (no doubt at the instigation of several provincial governments) to eliminate the mini separation of powers doctrine the courts have created out of section 96 through a constitutional amendment.[12] The proposal involved renaming the existing section 96, section 96A, and adding a new section 96B that would free provincial legislatures to allocate to provincially established administrative tribunals such adjudicative functions as they wished provided only that the decisions of such tribunals remained subject to judicial review by superior courts. Interestingly, and given the decision in *McEvoy*, significantly, the proposed new section 96B made no mention of Parliament and hence would not have eliminated the mini separation of powers doctrine insofar as it was concerned. In any case, the proposal generated very little support — or perhaps more accurately, very little interest — and it went nowhere. I have not heard of any suggestions in recent years that such a proposal is likely to be revived, this in spite of the fact that section 96 continues to generate a fair bit of litigation, and remains an obstacle to both orders of government insofar as their power to assign adjudicative functions to bodies other than section 96 courts is concerned.

I turn now to my critique of what the courts have done in this area. Part of this critique relates to problems with the *Residential Tenancies* test, the other part, and for me the more important part, to the whole way of thinking about section 96 that underlies that test. The problems with the test itself are numerous. Perhaps the most obvious is that it gives undue weight to history, and particularly to the year 1867. Important as that year is to Canadians, it is difficult to see why it should play such a critical role in resolving for all time what should be issues of constitutional principle. Another is that the test is too easily manipulated. Particularly at the first stage, a great deal turns on how one defines the adjudicative function in question, and the test leaves judges with a relatively free hand in this regard. Then there is Justice Wilson's holding in the *Sobeys* that only the four original provinces count for the purposes of applying the historical part of the test, unless these four provinces produce a tie, in which case one turns to the United Kingdom. As a westerner, there is something offensive about a constitutional law doctrine that has national application but is grounded in the histories of Ontario, Quebec, Nova Scotia and New Brunswick. As a Canadian, there is something equally offensive in the notion that issues of Canadian constitutional law should be resolved on the basis of British institutional history.

The problems do not rest solely with the first part of the test. In formulating the second part of the test — the "judicial" function in isolation part of the test — in the way in which it has, the Court appears almost to invite provincial legislatures to depart from the basic constitutional principles of the rule of law and due process when they assign adjudicative functions to provincially established administrative tribunals. Any test, in this or in any other area, that rewards our elected officials for acting in a manner inconsistent with such long standing and important values must be said to be seriously flawed. The third part of the test — the "judicial" function in its institutional setting part of the test — provides encouragement to legislative bodies looking to circumvent section 96 to make it appear from the way in which their legislation is drafted that an adjudicative function that might otherwise be vulnerable to challenge was being performed in an institutional setting in which that function was ancillary to larger administrative or policy goals. In other words, this part of the test is subject to manipulation as well, this time bylegislative bodies rather than by judges.

As numerous and as serious as these problems with the test are, they exist at the surface level. The real problem with the mini separation of powers doctrine that the courts have constructed out of section 96 lies at a much deeper level. What the courts have forgotten in developing this doctrine is the lesson that Professor Lederman taught us so well in his writings on Canadian constitutional law. That lesson is that legal doctrine in the area of constitutional law, however we formulate it, must be grounded in and hence explicable in terms of our basic constitutional values. The real problem with the *Residential Tenancies* test is that it is divorced from constitutional values. It is a purely descriptive test, one that asks what history tells us, whether or not the function viewed in isolation is a "judicial" function, and whether it retains that character when viewed in its institutional setting. In short, the test lacks normative content.

Related to this lack of normative content, and largely responsible for it, is the fact that in developing this doctrine the courts have tended to focus exclusively on section 96 and ignored the other provisions in the judicature component of the *Constitution Act, 1867*. Professor Lederman was surely right to argue, as he did in his 1956 piece, that section 96 was part of an integrated whole defined by sections 96 through 100 and designed to define some of the basic characteristics of the court system that Canada was to have.[13] Of this set of provisions, section 96 can hardly be said to be the most important. Section 99, which deals with security of tenure, and section 100, which deals with the financial security of judges, prescribed characteristics of this system that not only have very deep roots in the constitutional history out of which our system of government has evolved but that go to the very heart of that system. Moreover, these other provisions are no less susceptible of the kind of functional interpretation that the courts have given to section 96. It is just as easy to say that persons who perform the functions of superior court judges shall have the kind of security of tenure for which section 99 provides, and that persons who perform the functions of superior, district and county court judges shall have the kind of financial security for which section 100 provides. If a case can be made for a mini separation of powers doctrine in this country, and I believe that it can, that doctrine should be grounded not simply in section 96 but in all of sections 96 through 100.

Another troubling aspect of the way in which the courts have approached this area is their tendency to view it exclusively in terms of issues of power. In purely formal terms that tendency is understandable. Section 96 is about power — the power to appoint the judges of superior, district and county courts. Given the courts' focus on section 96, it is therefore almost inevitable that power — the power to appoint particular kinds of adjudicators — will feature in the analysis. This tendency goes beyond the formal. At the substantive level, section 96 cases are understood in terms of another kind of power — the power to adjudicate. The question in each case is which adjudicative body — the s. 96 court or the administrative tribunal — has the power to adjudicate the particular kind of dispute in question. And then in the *McEvoy* case one even finds reference being made to the interest of the legal profession in ensuring that the members of that profession will continue to have access to the most significant appointments within our dispute resolution system.[14] So, in a sense, one has the power of the bar being placed in opposition to the power of non-lawyers. The thinking process in this area therefore seems to be grounded very much in concerns about which institutions within society — the federal government, provincial governments, section 96 courts, administrative tribunals, and the bar — are entitled to exercise which powers. It is this emphasis on power and the allocation thereof between differentinstitutions within society that has no doubt led to the label "mini separation of powers" doctrine being attached to the law in this area.

What is troubling about this emphasis on power, at least to me, is that it encourages us either to ignore completely or to treat as essentially unimportant the interests of individual litigants looking to have their disputes resolved by government appointed adjudicators. My own view is that those interests lie at the very heart of what is at stake in this area. Real as the institutional interests may be — interests defined in terms of the desire to enhance or at least maintain certain kinds of power — it must be remembered that the ultimate goal of any system of dispute resolution, and hence of the institutions that comprise it, is to serve well those who make use of it. To the extent, therefore, that the doctrine in this area fails to take account of the interests of litigants, it misses the mark in a very fundamental sense.

That leads me to the concluding part of this paper, in which I propose to sketch out an alternative way of thinking about section 96 and the issues to which it has been understood to give rise. That alternative approach starts from the premise that it is the interests of litigants with which we should be primarily concerned. The question is one of rights — the rights of these litigants — not of power. The rights with which we are concerned are the rights to particular kinds of adjudicators, and indirectly, to a particular kind of justice. This approach also pejectq the primacy of section 96 and entails viewing sections 96-100 as an integrated whole in the way in which Professor Lederman viewed them. So viewed, these provisions give us the characteristics of a certain kind of adjudicator within our system, the judge of a superior, district or county court. Such an adjudicator was appointed by the federal order of government, was a member of the bar in the province in which he or she presides, has the security of tenure for which section 99 provides, and has the financial security for which section 100 provides. Of particular importance to the development of this alternative approach are the latter two provisions. For it is they that provide the normative content of this approach. What these two provisions speak to, and what they guarantee in the strongest terms known to our system of government, is the value of arbitral independence.

Connecting these three threads together — the concern about the rights of litigants, viewing section 96 as part of an integrated whole, and focussing upon the value of arbitral independence — we can generate the question to which this alternative approach would give rise. That question is *given the nature of the dispute between the litigants in question, are they entitled to an adjudicator of a kind for which sections 96-100 provide, and in particular, are they entitled to an adjudicator drawn from the bar and with the kind of independence for which sections 99 and 100 provide?*

This alternative approach would not, it should be noted, be entirely without support from the case law. The Privy Council, in one of its better known decisions in this area, *Toronto v. York Township*, situated section 96 very much within the larger context of the judicature provisions of the then *B.N.A. Act, 1867* and drew explicit attention to the value of judicial independence embodied in sections 99 and 100.[15] More recently, in *McEvoy*, the Supreme Court of Canada did the same.[16] And in an even more recent decision of the Federal Court of Appeal, *Rifou v. C.I.B.C.*, Mr. Justice Mahoney at least implicitly suggests that the existing doctrine in this area be replaced by a test grounded in the value of judicial independence.[17]

Support for this alternative approach can also be found in some of the decisions generated by section 11(d) of the *Charter*, which explicitly grants to "any person charged with an offence" the right "to be presumed innocent until proven guilty according to law in a fair and public hearing by an "independent and impartial tribunal". In giving meaning to the latter phrase, the Supreme Court of Canada has noted the existence of sections 99 and 100 of the *Constitution Act, 1867* and described them as providing the maximum degree of arbitral independence known to our legal system.[18] Not all decision makers within that system, the Court has held, need to have their independence protected to quite the same degree; provincial court judges can be held to satisfy the requirements of independence and impartiality prescribed by section 11(d) even though they do not enjoy the same security of tenure and financial security as section 96 court judges. Implicit in this line of reasoning clearly seems to be the proposition that section 96 court judges, and the independence they enjoy, are required only for certain special kinds of adjudicative tasks.

However, the case for adopting this alternative approach to our mini separation of powers doctrine cannot be made on the basis that it represents a better reading of the jurisprudence. That case must be made, as I have attempted to make it above, on the basis that this approach provides the doctrine with the normative content that it currently lacks, and moreover, that it does so on the basis of a better reading of section 96 than that doctrine currently reflects.

What would be the practical consequences of adopting this alternative approach? Given the willingness of the Supreme Court of Canada in its s. 11(d) decisions to tolerate lower standards of judicial independence for provincial court judges than those reflected in sections 96-100, I suspect that this alternative approach would result in very few kinds of disputes having to be adjudicated by section 96 court judges. Nevertheless, one could imagine the Court holding that those *Criminal*

Code offences like sedition and treason, in which the interests of the accused are in a very direct sense placed in opposition to those of the government, and hence in respect of which the need for independence is especially acute, would have to be adjudicated by such judges. In other words, those accused of such offences would be accorded the right to be tried by such judges. One could easily imagine the same right being given to those seeking a final determination as to the nature and scope of the jurisdiction of an inferior court or an administrative tribunal. Hence, this approach would lead to the same result as that arrived at in *Crevier*, albeit for somewhat different reasons. And it is to be expected that litigants raising a constitutional challenge to the validity of some form of governmental action would be given the right under this approach to have section 96 court judges make the final determination on those challenges. It may be possible to extend this list somewhat further.

It would, however, remain a fairly short list. To some this would be an attractive feature of this alternative approach, to others an unattractive feature. To those in the latter camp, I would point out that even under the existing approach, very few functions have been held to be section 96 court functions. I would also point out that this new approach would not be the only technique for protecting the societal interest in arbitral independence. It would be supplemented by a range of other techniques. Mention has already been made of section 11(d) of the *Charter*. Mention should also be made of section 7 of the *Charter*. The right to an independent and impartial arbitrator is clearly a principle of fundamental justice; hence, litigants can invoke section 7 whenever an adjudicator is in a position through his or her decision making authority to deprive them of their life, liberty or security of the person. It is important to bear in mind section 2(e) of the *Canadian Bill of Rights* and that provision's counterparts in some of the provincial bills of rights. Section 2(e) protects "the right to a fair hearing in accordance with the principles of fundamental justice for the determination of [a person's] rights and obligations".

This provision, through its reference both to a fair hearing and to the principles of fundamental justice, protects the right to an independent and impartial arbiter, and it will do so in a broader range of contexts than would section 7. That is because that right is not contingent under section 2(e), as it is under section 7 of the *Charter*, upon a deprivation of the right to life, liberty and security of the person; the right attaches under section 2(e) whenever a determination is being made about an individual's rights and obligations.

Then, of course, there is the common law. There can be little doubt now that lack of sufficient independence from the executive branch of government can be invoked in support of a claim of reasonable apprehension of bias or, as Heald J.A. put it in a recent case in the immigration area, that "the right of independence is included in the rules of natural justice".[19] While it is true that judges have been somewhat reluctant to make a finding of reasonable apprehension of bias on this basis, and while it is also true that the common law can be overridden by carefully worded statutory provisions, that body of law retains considerable potential as a vehicle for protecting this value.

Let me close with some speculation on the reaction that Professor Lederman would have had to this alternative approach. I suspect, given what he wrote about our mini separation of powers doctrine, that he would be concerned that this approach would result in too much being given away, that the core of jurisdiction guaranteed to the superior courts would, in other words, be too small. He might, however, have been placated at least somewhat by the fact that sections 11(d) and 7 of the *Charter*, as well as statutory bills of rights and the common law, were available to play a supporting role. He would also, I suspect, see the emphasis on arbitral independence as timely, given the controversy that has accompanied many appointments to administrative tribunals over the last decade or so.[20] Be that as it may, I am certain that he would see merit in the fact that this approach is based on the kind of integrated view of sections 96-100 for which he argued so persuasively and, even more importantly, that it is grounded in and reflects a commitment to one of our basic constitutional values. The fact that that value, judicial independence, was one to which he devoted a good deal of time and energy as a scholar would, I suspect, add to its appeal.

NOTES

1. W.R. Lederman, "The Independence of the Judiciary" (1956), 34 Can. Bar Rev. 769-809 and 1139-1179. His discussion of the mini separation of powers doctrine is found at 1158-1177.
2. For an extended discussion of this body of doctrine, see P.W. Hogg, *Constitutional Law of Canada* (3rd ed., 1992), at 184-200 and 498-503.
3. [1981] 1 S.C.R. 714.
4. The test is developed *ibid.* at 728-736.
5. [1986] 2 S.C.R. 226, at 250.
6. *McEvoy v. A.-G. N.B.*, [1983] 1 S.C.R. 704.
7. See, e.g., *R. v. Trimarchi* (1987), 63 O.R. (2d) 515 (C.A.).
8. See *Re Young Offenders Act*, [1991] 1 S.C.R. 252 and *Chrysler Canada Ltd. v. Canada (Competition Tribunal)*, [1992] 2 S.C.R. 394.
9. *Sobeys Stores Ltd. v. Yeomans*, [1989] 1 S.C.R. 238.
10. *Ibid.* at 289.
11. *Crevier v. A.-G. Quebec*, [1981] 1 S.C.R. 220.
12. *The Constitution of Canada: A Suggested Amendment Relating to Provincial Administrative Tribunals* (Dept. of Justice, Ottawa, 1983).
13. *Supra*, note 1, at 1172.
14. *Supra*, note 6, at 720.
15. [1938] A.C. 415, at 426.

16. *Supra*, note 6, at 719-720.
17. [1986] 3 F.C. 486, at 493.
18. *Valente v. The Queen*, [1985] 2 S.C.R. 673.
19. *Mohammed v. Canada (Minister of Employment and Immigration)*, [1989] 2 F.C. 363 (App. Div.), at 386. See generally, S. Comtois, "*L'évolution des principes d'indépendence et d'impartialité quasi-judiciaire: récents développements*" (1992), 6 C.J.A.L.P. 187.
20. See generally *The Independence of Federal Administrative Tribunals and Agencies in Canada* (C.B.A. Task Force Report, 1990).

Separate but not Apart:
The Role of the Courts in Canada's
Post-Charter Democracy

Martha Jackman[1]

I am pleased to have been invited to speak at this symposium in Professor Lederman's honour. I only knew Professor Lederman indirectly, as an elder statesperson of constitutional law, hovering over my undergraduate studies here at Queen's and later in Toronto. However, I am certainly among those who have tried to marshall his writings in support of my own claims, with the notion that this would somehow add to their credibility and persuasiveness. I hope that my presentation this morning will be in the spirit of his work, since what I want to do is to try to look forward to see how our constitutional text can be read to contribute to better politics and better government.

In principle, the separation of powers between the executive, the legislature and the courts is an important feature of Canadian constitutional law. As former Chief Justice Dickson explained in his 1985 judgment in *Fraser v. P.S.S.R.B.*:

> There is in Canada a separation of powers among the three branches of government — the legislature, the executive and the judiciary. In broad terms, the role of the judiciary is, of course, to interpret and apply the law; the role of the legislature is to decide upon and enunciate policy; the role of the executive is to administer and implement that policy.[2]

In practice, however, and especially as compared to the United States, the separation of powers in Canada exists in a highly attenuated form. Owing largely to competing principles of responsible government, the executive exercises enormous control over the activities of the legislature, at both the federal and the provincial levels.[3]

For whatever reason, most commentary on the separation of powers in Canada has overlooked the executive's dominance over the legislative branch and has focused instead on the role of the judiciary. In the pre-*Charter* era, as reflected in Professor Lederman's earlier writings on this subject, constitutional safeguards against executive and legislative interferences with judicial independence were the primary topic of interest.[4] More recently, the concern of constitutional scholars has shifted, with those from both ends of the ideological spectrum focusing on the perceived threat to parliamentary democracy posed by growing judicial incursions into thelegislative realm as a result of *Charter* litigation.[5]

Critics argue that, because of the contingent nature of rights and the lack of objective standards in this area, judges engaged in *Charter* review will substitute their own values for those of elected legislatures. In enforcing rights, courts will effectively dictate public policy, forcing governments to spend public monies in ways they did not plan or choose. In addition to eroding public confidence in the independence and integrity of the judiciary, it is claimed that this usurpation of policy making by the courts will lead to an abdication of responsibility by the legislatures, and to frustration and eventual apathy in voters. In short, by transferring social and economic policy making from elected legislatures to appointed and unaccountable courts, *Charter* review is seen as inconsistent with basic democratic principles, and therefore highly undesirable.

In my view, however, this issue warrants rethinking. In particular, the current focus on the separation of powers between the legislature and the courts needs to be balanced by a re-examination of the relationship among all three branches of government, and by a reconsideration of whether the courts can, through *Charter* review, enhance, rather than detract from, the quality of democratic decision-making by the executive and the legislative branches alike.

In the following discussion I will argue that, to the extent judicial review on *Charter* grounds meets fundamental democratic objectives of encouraging greater participation — both individual and collective — in all aspects of government decision-making, it is to be sought-after rather than rejected. This approach, it must be emphasized, is fully consistent with the underlying purposes of the *Charter* which are to ensure, as Justice Dickson confirmed in his decision in *R. v. Oakes*,[6] that Canadian society is both free *and* democratic.

In order to support my claim that judicial review on *Charter* grounds has the potential to contribute to democratic objectives, I will examine two recent cases from the social welfare context: *Conrad v. County of Halifax*,[7] and *Dartmouth/ Halifax County Regional Housing Authority v. Sparks*.[8] After briefly reviewing the facts of the two cases, I will focus on deficiencies in the decision-making processes at issue in each case — deficiencies which deprive those affected of a meaningful opportunity to participate in decisions which have serious implications for them. I will then consider how judicial review on *Charter* grounds might operate to correct these flaws, whether at a procedural or at a broader substantive level, and so improvethe democratic tenor of decision-making.

THE FACTS OF THE CASES

Lorraine Conrad separated from her husband, Curtis Conrad, because of his alcoholism and physical abusiveness, in early January 1989. Later that month, she applied for municipal social assistance benefits from the City of Halifax, for her and her three dependent children (ages 7, 15 and 18), to supplement her monthly income of $65 in family allowance and $1 in spousal maintenance. She received monthly municipal benefits of $712 until August 30, 1989, at which time she was informed that her benefits were being terminated, on the grounds that she and her husband had resumed cohabitation.

Irma Sparks, a black single mother of three (ages 8, 16 and 22), lived with her two youngest children in a subsidized housing unit in Dartmouth, which the family had occupied continuously since December, 1980. On May 1, 1990, she received notice from her landlord, the Dartmouth/Halifax County Regional Housing Authority, that her tenancy would be terminated at the end of the month. No reasons were given for her eviction.

THE LACK OF PROCEDURAL SAFEGUARDS

The first major flaw in the decision-making processes in *Conrad* and *Sparks* relates to the serious lack of procedural safeguards provided upon termination of benefits, which effectively deprived Lorraine Conrad and Irma Sparks of a meaningful opportunity to participate in the individualized decisions affecting them. This situation is especially objectionable in view of the severe consequences of the decision in each case: for Lorraine Conrad, the loss of income needed to support her and her children; for Irma Sparks, the loss of her family's housing.

Among the procedural shortcomings in the two cases are the inadequacy of notice, the failure to provide reasons, and the failure to provide a pre-termination hearing. Lorraine Conrad received notice that her social assistance benefits were being terminated effective immediately. Irma Sparks received one month's notice of eviction. In neither case did officials contact, or enter into any sort of discussions with, the two women prior to the termination. In *Conrad*, no explanation was provided for the finding that the couple had resumed cohabitation, or that the husband was making any financial contribution to the household. In *Sparks*, no disclosure was made of the grounds for Irma Sparks' eviction.

No provision was made for a pre-termination hearing in either case. Neither woman had an opportunity to question officials, to refute allegations, or to respond to the reasons given for the termination prior to its becoming effective. Instead, each woman had to rely on a formal post-termination appeal process to challenge the correctness of the decision. As the United States Supreme Court held in its landmark decision in *Goldberg v. Kelly*, such a procedure presents particular difficulties for social welfare recipients:

> Welfare provides the means to obtain essential food, clothing, housing, and medical care .... Thus ... termination of aid pending resolution of a controversy over eligibility may deprive an eligible recipient of the very means by which to live while he waits. Since he lacks independent resources his situation becomes immediately desperate. His need to concentrate upon finding the means for daily subsistence, in turn, adversely affects his ability to seek redress from the welfare bureaucracy.[9]

The same could as easily be said of those evicted from subsidized housing, who must then begin a difficult search for affordable housing within the private rental market.

THE LACK OF ACCOUNTABILITY

In addition to failing to provide adequate procedural safeguards, the decision-making processes in *Conrad* and *Sparks* are also highly unaccountable, due in large part to the wide grant of discretion to officials in each case. In *Conrad*, the Nova Scotia *Social Assistance Act*[10] imposes an obligation on the municipality to provide social assistance in the barest of terms. Section 9(1) of the Act provides merely that: "Subject to this Act and the regulations the social services committee shall furnish assistance to all persons in need, as defined by the social services committee, who reside in the municipal unit". "Person in need" is defined in section 4(d) of the Act simply as, "a person who, by reason of adverse conditions, requires assistance in the form of money, goods or services".

The regulations under the Act provide little further direction. Section 2(1) grants the Director of the Social Services the power to, "determine the immediate and continuing eligibility of each applicant", to "provide assistance in accordance with the provisions of the Act, these regulations and the municipal social services policy", and to "ensure that the applicant has no other reasonable source of income which can be used for his financial needs". Thus, the legislation delegates to the executive virtually unfettered decision-making authority (exercisable in this case by the social services committee), in terms of the beneficiaries of the legislative regime, the type, amount and conditions of assistance, the process for determining eligibility, the grounds upon which benefits can be terminated, and the appeal process following such termination.

The consequences of such a wide grant of discretion are illustrated by what actually happened in *Conrad*. There, the municipal welfare worker determined that Lorraine Conrad and her husband had resumed cohabitation, and terminated Lorraine's benefits, on the basis of a note written by a neighbour (described by the welfare worker herself as "a chronic complainer") stating his belief that the Conrads were living together. At the time of termination, the welfare worker had no evidence of the husband's financial contribution to the family, and so was unable to make any real determination of need. Instead, Lorraine Conrad was faced with a summary termination of her benefits without being informed of the basis for the decision (i.e., the complaint from the neighbour), and without being provided any opportunity to respond.

In *Sparks*, section 25(2) of the Nova Scotia *Residential Tenancies Act*[11] expressly excludes subsidized housing from the provisions of the *Act* thereby enabling public housing officials to exercise total discretion in their decision to evict a subsidized tenant, and for what reasons. Irma Sparks's tenancy was terminated after twelve years, upon 30 days notice, without reasons. Only after she made an application to see her file under provincial access to information legislation did she learn that her eviction was the result of allegations that her 22 year old son, who no longer lived with her, was selling drugs in her housing complex when he came to visit her. The summary treatment accorded to Irma Sparks and other subsidized tenants is in sharp contrast to the legislative provisions in favour of private sector tenants, who are guaranteed three months notice of eviction, and who after five years can only be evicted for default of their obligations under the lease.[12]

THE DELEGATION OF DECISION-MAKING AUTHORITY

The vast discretion granted to the welfare officials in *Conrad*, and to the public housing officials in *Sparks*, is symptomatic of a more substantive problem in the decision-making processes in these cases, that is, the wholesale delegation by the legislature, of both the power to make individualised decisions, and the power to formulate the policy upon which such decisions are based. Contrary to Justice Dickson's description of the underlying principles of the separation of powers in Canadian law, not only policy implementation but also policy formulation are both exercised by parliamentary delegates and sub-delegates within the executive branch.

This delegation of decision-making authority deprives those affected of the ability to participate in individualised decisions affecting them, and to participate in the broader process of policy formation. Thus, it is extremely difficult to determine who, in fact, has the authority to formulate which policies, and on what bases. The exact parameters of the policy making authority are rarely articulated in law or regulation. If at all, they are generally found in informal policy directives, or simply in unwritten practices and procedures. The effect of this informal and invisible delegation of authority is that, in their policy making activities, delegated decision-makers are insulated from, and so unaccountable to, those who are most directly affected by their decisions.

Interposed between the Nova Scotia legislature and Lorraine Conrad, for instance, are the municipality, the social services committee, the municipal welfare bureaucracy, and the individual welfare worker. Adding to Lorraine Conrad's inability to challenge the factual basis of the decision to terminate her benefits is the difficulty of challenging the "man in the house" rule, upon which that decision is based. Not only is it unclear at what level and by whom the policy was formulated, it is also difficult to determine who has the authority to modify it. Irma Sparks faces a similar difficulty in challenging factual assumptions about her relationship with her eldest son, and also the policy whereby drug use in public housing is to be controlled by imposing responsibility, through threat of eviction, on entire families for the activities of their individual members.

Further, delegated decision-makers are also insulated from, and unaccountable to, the very legislatures who granted them their authority. As many commentators have noted, delegation of legislative authority is a pervasive feature of Canadian government.[13] Many of the decisions which bear most heavily on individual well being, in a number of contexts, including welfare, health and safety, immigration, prisons, and the environment, are made by legislative delegates. Recipients of delegated power range from individual bureaucrats within government departments, to Cabinet, independent administrative boards and agencies, municipalities, hospitals, and other government officials and quasi-governmental bodies.

Because of the scope and frequency of such delegations, and the lack of supervision or ongoing legislative oversight, it is highly unlikely that a wrong decision in one individual case, or even in a long series of cases, will be held up to legislative scrutiny. It is also unlikely that policies, developed by delegated decision-makers as a basis for their decisions, will be reviewed for their conformity to legislative objectives. Thus, it is extremely improbable that the welfare officials in *Conrad*, or the housing officials in *Sparks*, will be called to account to the legislature either for their decision to terminate the two women's benefits, or for the particular policies upon which the decisions were made.

THE UNDER-REPRESENTATION OF AFFECTED INTERESTS

Clearly, social welfare recipients and public housing tenants are not well represented within the executive branch, or in social welfare and public housing bureaucracies. Even more significant, however, they are not well represented within Parliament and the legislatures themselves. Thus, at the source of the flaws described above in the decision-making processes in *Conrad* and *Sparks* is, arguably, the under-representation of the interests of those affected by decisions among those empowered to make the decisions and policies under challenge.

For the poor, among whom social welfare beneficiaries and subsidized housing tenants are two prominent groups, the problem is circular: the political process is largely inaccessible to them, they have lower rates of political participation, and electoral politics are generally unresponsive to their needs and demands.[14] The National Anti-Poverty Organization describes this situation as follows:

> There are obviously many important barriers that restrict the access and the participation of lower income Canadians in Canada's democratic political process. A wide range of financial and class barriers, for example, limit the possibilities for poor Canadians who wish to run as candidates for election .... As a result, our Members of Parliament are overwhelmingly representative of the privileged white, male non-disabled middle to upper class segment of our society. On the other hand ... lower income Canadians are barely visible in the elected and non-elected chambers of Parliament. Partly as a result, many lower income Canadians have relatively little faith in the ability or desire of our elected officials to represent their interests.[15]

The outcome of this lack of legislative representation is evident in both *Conrad* and *Sparks*. It is hard to imagine that the vagueness and bureaucratic discretion manifest in the welfare regime at issue in *Conrad* would be tolerated in any other area of legislative or regulatory activity. In *Sparks*, the impact of the marginal status of subsidized tenants is even more overt, as reflected by their outright exclusion from the ordinary protection of provincial residential tenancies legislation. In each case, laws and decision-making processes reflect and perpetuate the lack of legislative accountability to, and representation of, those affected.

PARTICIPATION IN INDIVIDUALISED DECISION-MAKING

How might *Charter*-based judicial review ameliorate the undemocratic quality of the government decision-making processes at issue in *Conrad* and *Sparks*? First, recognition by the courts of a "security of the person" related interest under section 7 of the *Charter*,[16] in the continuation of social assistance benefits in *Conrad*, and in continued occupancy of subsidized housing in *Sparks*, would clearly ensure greater participation in individualised decision-making in these areas.

Reading section 7 to protect such basic welfare entitlements is consistent with the broader interpretive context within which the Supreme Court has emphasized the *Charter* must be read,[17] including prevailing conceptions of the relationship between the individual, the community and the state, long standing Canadian social welfare traditions, and Canada's extensive international commitments in the field of social and economic rights.[18] In the particular cases of Lorraine Conrad and Irma Sparks, the negative impact of a termination of benefits on their security of the person is evident and direct. As discussed above, Lorraine Conrad is left, with no prior notice, to support herself and her three children on an income of less than $70 per month; Irma Sparks must, within a month, find alternate non-subsidized housing for herself and her two children on an income of less than $800 per month.

Judicial recognition that basic welfare-related interests, such as those at issue in *Conrad* and *Sparks*, are protected under the right to security of the person would enhance the quality of decision-making by ensuring that any decision to terminate benefits had to meet the requirements of "fundamental justice". In procedural terms, the guarantee of fundamental justice entails a number of safeguards, all of which contribute to greater participatory opportunities in decision-making. These include the right to adequate notice of the decision being taken, the right to full disclosure of the reasons for the decision, an opportunity to respond to and discuss the decision with the person responsible for making it, and the right to appeal the decision, including the means necessary to exercise such a right.[19]

Procedural guarantees of this nature would have enabled Lorraine Conrad to dispute her neighbour's unsubstantiated claims that her husband had resumed cohabitation with her, as well as the suggestion that he was making any financial contribution to the family, before her benefits were terminated. Irma Sparks would also have had an opportunity, before the eviction notice became effective, to challenge the suggestion that she was responsible for, or could control, her 22 year old son's activities, particularly when he no longer lived with her.

By ensuring a better level of participation in the decisions in question, the procedural safeguards outlined above satisfy the more traditional objectives related to natural justice which section 7 is intended to promote. However, process-based guarantees of this nature also respond to broader democratic ideals of justice, according to which the legitimacy of public decision-making depends upon the participation of those whose interests are at stake.

PARTICIPATION IN THE POLICY-MAKING PROCESS

In addition to providing better procedural safeguards, and thereby enhancing participatory opportunities in individualised decision-making by legislative delegates, judicial review on *Charter* grounds also has the potential for remedying more substantive flaws in the policy making process at work in *Conrad* and *Sparks*.

The fact situations in *Conrad* and *Sparks* make it clear that the section 7 guarantee of fundamental justice must extend beyond the individualized decision-making context, and into the broader regulatory and policy making realm, if it is to provide effective protection for the interests at stake. The provision of procedural safeguards only after a decision has been made offers inadequate protection in the *Conrad* and *Sparks* cases because it places the entire burden of challenging the decision on the individual victims, after the injury has actually taken place. Procedural safeguards alone are also insufficient because they fail to allow for substantive challenges to the actual policies upon which the adverse decisions are founded.

On that basis it can be argued that principles of fundamental justice require collective participation by affected individuals and groups during the policy-making process itself.[20] Collective participation in policy-making is necessary in order to promote greater accountability, to overcome existing barriers to representation, and to ensure that the interests of under- or unrepresented groups, such as welfare beneficiaries and subsidized housing tenants, are taken into account. In other words, the "man in the house rule" in *Conrad*, and the eviction policy in *Sparks* can be found to violate section 7 because social welfare recipients and subsidized housing tenants were not provided with any meaningful opportunity to participate in the process whereby these policies were formulated and put into place.

PARTICIPATION IN THE LEGISLATIVE PROCESS

Finally, it can be argued that decisions such as the ones at issue in *Conrad* and *Sparks* violate section 7 because the legislative process itself fails to ensure participation of the affected groups. As suggested above, the vague and highly discretionary character of the social assistance legislation in *Conrad*, the express omission of subsidized housing from residential tenancies laws in *Sparks*, and the corresponding lack of control over the legislative delegates in both cases, reflect the absence of social welfare recipients and subsidized tenants from the legislature. Theinsecurity experienced by Lorraine Conrad, Irma Sparks, and other social welfare beneficiaries in a similar position, a result of the procedural and substantive deficiencies outlined above, facilitates and reinforces that legislative exclusion. By undermining their personal dignity, their sense of personal competence, and control over their lives, these deficiencies in the social assistance regimes upon which they depend to live compromise seriously the ability of individuals to participate as full and equal members in Canadian political life.

In the absence of evidence of affirmative attempts to secure the participation and representation of these historically unrepresented groups in the legislative process, it can be argued that failure by the legislature to provide adequate statutory safeguards when their interests are at risk violates section 7 principles of fundamental justice. Judicial review for the effects of legislative inattention or exclusion would mean that the summary procedures for terminating social assistance benefits in *Conrad*, and for evicting subsidized tenants in *Sparks*, offend section 7 of the *Charter*, because they reflect and contribute to the continued marginalization of these groups.

Like *Charter*-based scrutiny to guarantee participation in individualised decision-making, and to increase participation in the broader policy making process, judicial review for the effects of legislative inattention or exclusion would promote fundamental democratic objectives by encouraging the further democratization of the legislative process itself.

ENHANCED DEMOCRATIC DECISION-MAKING

From the foregoing discussion I hope that it has become clear that judicial review of executive and legislative action on *Charter* grounds has the potential to enhance rather than, necessarily, to detract from the quality of democratic decision-making at all levels of government. By interpreting section 7 principles of fundamental justice to require meaningful participation by those whose interests are affected in individualized decision-making, in broader policy making within the executive branch, and in the legislative process itself, the courts can provide an important avenue for challenges to anti-democratic tendencies in our current parliamentary system.

This being said, however, Professor Lederman's writings on the role of the courts, and more recent works by the *Charter* critics about the dangers of judicial review, highlight important institutional barriers to the existing ability of the courts to act in the way I have proposed. In order for judicial review on *Charter* grounds to reflect, rather than undermine democratic values, significant measures must be taken to enhance values of participation, accountability and representation in the courts' own decision-making processes.

At an attitudinal level, contrary to what the Supreme Court suggested in its decision in *Dolphin Delivery*,[21] judges must acknowledge that the courts are an integral part of, rather than apart from, our government. At a more practical level, courts and judicial processes need to be reviewed for their procedural and financial accessibility, as well as for their capacity to be understood, in order to ensure that all segments of the community can participate in their processes. Much greater vigilance and openness in judicial discipline and self-regulatory proceedings is necessary in order to promote a higher degree of judicial accountability. Finally, better representation must be guaranteed through further reform of the judicial appointments system, to secure a more representative and diverse judiciary, and through continuing judicialeducation for those already on the bench.

In summary, provided judges are attuned to this potential, *Charter* review can operate to promote democratic values; it can provide an opportunity to challenge existing meanings of democracy, and to take those meanings back into politics and government; and in so doing it can help to ensure democratic participation in all aspects of public decision-making. Judicial review for these purposes is, I would argue, an appropriate, indeed a necessary, role for the courts in Canada's post-*Charter* democracy.

NOTES

1. The author wishes to thank Ruth Sullivan for helpful comments on an earlier draft of this paper, and her daughter, Elizabeth, for her patience while it was being written.
2. [1985] 2 S.C.R. 455 at 479; see also *Operation Dismantle v. The Queen*, [1985] 1 S.C.R. 441 at 491.
3. This feature of Canadian government has led some, such as Professor Peter Hogg, to question whether the doctrine has any real place in Canadian law; see for example P.W. Hogg, *Constitutional Law of Canada*, 3rd ed. (Toronto: Carswell, 1993) 184-5, 243.
4. See for example W.R. Lederman, "The Independence of the Judiciary" in *Continuing Canadian Constitutional Dilemmas — Essays on the Constitutional History, Public Law and Federal System of Canada* (Toronto: Butterworths, 1981) 109.
5. See for example J. Frémont, "Les tribunaux et la *Charte*: le pouvoir d'ordonner la dépense de fonds publics en matières sociales et économiques" (1991) 36 McGill L.J. 1323; A. Petter, "The Politics of the Charter" (1986) 8 Sup. Ct L. Rev 473; R.I. Cheffins & P.A. Johnson, *The Revised Canadian Constitution — Politics as Law* (Toronto: McGraw-Hill Ryerson, 1986); D.A. Schmeiser, "The Case Against the Entrenchment of a Canadian Bill of Rights" (1973) 1 Dalhousie L.J. 15.
6. [1986] 1 S.C.R. 103 at 136.
7. (11 August 1993), C.H. No. 70286 (N.S.S.Ct.).
8. (1992) 112 N.S.R. (2d) 389 (N.S.Co.Ct.), rev'd (2 March 1993) S.C.A. No. 02681 (N.S.C.A.). The author wishes to thank Vince Calderhead of Metro Community Law Clinic (Halifax) for copies of pleadings and unpublished judgments in the *Sparks* and *Conrad* cases.
9. 397 U.S. 254 (1970) at 262-63.
10. R.S.N.S. 1989, c. 432.
11. R.S.N.S. 1989, c. 401.
12. *Residential Tenancies Act, supra*, s. 10.
13. See for example J.R. Mallory, "Curtailing Divine Right: The Control of Delegated Legislation in Canada" in O.P. Dwivedi, ed., *The Administrative State in Canada* (Toronto: University of Toronto Press, 1982) 131; J.R. Mallory, "Can Parliament Control the Regulatory Process?" (Autumn 1983) *Can. Parliamentary Rev.* 6; T. D'Aquino, B. Doern & C. Blair, *Parliamentary Democracy in Canada — Issues for Reform* (Toronto: Methuen, 1983).

14. For a discussion of this problem, see generally National Anti-Poverty Organization, *Poor People and the Federal Electoral System: Barriers to Participation* (Ottawa: National Anti-Poverty Organization, May 1990); R.J. VanLoon & M.S. Whittington, *The Canadian Political System — Environment, Structure and Process* (Toronto: McGraw-Hill Ryerson, 1987) at 154; W. Mishler, *Political Participation in Canada* (Toronto: Macmillan, 1979) at 88-95.

15. N.A.P.O., *Poor People and the Federal Electoral System, supra,* at 3.

16. Section 7 of the *Charter* provides that: "Everyone has the right to life, liberty and security of the person and the right not to be deprived thereof except in accordance with the principles of fundamental justice."

17. *R. v. Big M Drug Mart Ltd.,* [1985] 1 S.C.R. 295 at 344; *Hunter et al. v. Southam Inc.,* [1984] 2 S.C.R. 145 at 155.

18. For a discussion of this context, and further elaboration of the argument that welfare rights are guaranteed under section 7 of the *Charter,* see M. Jackman, "The Protection of Welfare Rights Under the Charter" (1988) 20 Ottawa L. Rev. 257; see also J.D. Whyte, "Fundamental Justice: The Scope and Application of Section 7 of the Charter" (1983) 13 Man. L.J. 455; I. Morrison, "Security of the Person and the Person in Need: Section 7 of the Charter and the Right to Welfare" (1988) 4 J.L. & Social Pol'y 1; I. Johnstone, "Section 7 of the Charter and Constitutionally Protected Welfare" (1988) 46 U.T. Fac. L. Rev. 1.

19. For a discussion of the procedural content of section 7, see for example P. Garant, "Fundamental Rights and Fundamental Justice" in G.-A. Beaudoin & E. Ratushny, eds,*The Canadian Charter of Rights and Freedoms,* 2d ed. (Toronto: Carswell, 1989) 331.

20. For an elaboration of this argument see M. Jackman, "Rights and Participation: The Use of the Charter to Supervise the Regulatory Process" (1990) 4 C.J.A.L.P. 23.

21. *Retail, Wholesale and Department Store Union, Local 580 v. Dolphin Delivery Ltd.,* [1986] 2 S.C.R. 573.

PART THREE

EQUALITY RIGHTS

Equality in a Post Modern Time

Diana Majury

I too am very pleased to be here, even though I follow Lynn Smith as more of the pessimist on this panel. I have entitled my talk "Equality in A Post Modern Time". I have done so in order to give me an excuse for having no theme or thesis for my talk. This is not for want of trying, but struggle as I might I have been unable to find, and unable to impose, any order on the equality decisions I have been reading. So I have adopted the post modern context to give me permission to talk about some of the interrelated pieces that I see in the equality rights area without feeling that I have to try to make coherent sense of it.

In a post modern time equality may be a quintessentially post modern concept. I say this while enjoying the irony of using a word denoting essence in conjunction with anti-essentialist post modernism. It is one of the ironies of post modernism that it is very definitive in its lack of definitiveness. I invoke the post modern context as someone who does not define herself as a post modernist. In fact I am quite critical of much of what I understand post modernism to be about and even more critical of much of it that I find largely incomprehensible. At the same time, I think there is plenty in post modernism to challenge us, to draw on, and to think about.

Post modernism and the uncertain state of equality in the legal and larger social and political contexts are very much functions and reflections of our times. It is this uncertainty and its implications, both positive and negative, that I want to explore here this afternoon.

Perhaps the most post modern feature of equality is its indeterminacy. It is a term that is largely devoid of meaning. Thus it is that we have to fairly overtly read meaning into the term virtually every time it is used. In so doing, of course, we read in, from, and with all of our knowledge and experience, our biases and preconceptions and our stereotypes and prejudices. Thus, while equality is a place from which stereotypes and prejudice can be challenged, it is at the same time a place where stereotypes and prejudices can be reinforced and perpetuated. Justice

Linden in his dissent in *Egan*, one of the gay "spousal benefit" cases, said, "It would be paradoxical indeed if a decision under s.15 were itself to be based on prejudice and stereotyping."[1] I assume that he made that point because he recognized the problem in the majority judgment. This reliance upon stereotypes in the name of equality is, I think a central paradox of equality and one of the serious risks involved in bringing or responding to a s. 15 *Charter* challenge. This of course means that it matters more and more who is making these decisions, that is who is doing the reading in. Judicial appointments are equality issues on a number of levels which we heard about from Martha Jackman.

With respect to stereotypes and prejudice as the foundation of s.15 decisions, I think that age discrimination cases provide some of the most obvious examples, possibly because age discrimination is so invisible and/or so accepted, and seen as so "natural" in our society. The quote that Lynn Smith read from Madam Justice MacLaughlin as to why Sue Rodriguez's case was not about equality, "I am of the view that this is not at base a case about discrimination under s.15 of *Canadian Charter of Rights and Freedoms*, and that to treat it as such may deflect the equality jurisprudence from the true focus of s.15 ... to remedy or prevent discrimination against groups subject to stereotyping, historical disadvantage and political and social prejudice inCanadian society"[2], reflects the same point with respect to the invisibility of disability discrimination. Our discrimination against people with disabilities is so engrained, so natural, that we are unable to even contemplate it as discrimination. It is as Simone de Beauvoir said, "one of the ruses of oppression is to camouflage itself behind a natural situation since, after all, one cannot revolt against nature".[3]

The majority decision in *McKinney*[4], one of the mandatory retirement cases, invokes, both explicitly and implicitly, the stereotypical correlation between aging and declining ability, accompanied by the paternalism of allegedly saving people over 65 from the embarrassment of performance reviews. In the *Rosen* case[5], the Tax Court of Canada held that the definition of earned income for the purposes of RRSP contributions did not make distinctions on the basis of age, infirmity or lack of resources, as if somehow the three are synonymous. In addition, the Court in *Rosen* made the statement that the definition of income applies equally to all tax payers, inferring that such equal treatment means that the provision is not discriminatory. *This* in November of 1992. While some judges are overreading Andrews[6], it is not clear whether other judges have read it at all. This accords with Lynn Smith's analysis in terms of judges not recognizing the potential disparate impact.

At the other end of the age spectrum, is the decision in *Lister and Lister*[7], also from the Tax Court of Canada. The case involved a s.15 challenge to the refusal of a GST tax credit to persons under the age of 19. While this differential treatment may or may not constitute discrimination that may or not be justified, the court's finding, with no real discussion on the point, that people under the age of 19 are not members of a discrete and insular minority suffering stereotyping, historical disadvantage, or vulnerability to social and political pressure, would deny young people the age equality protections of s.15.

Now I want to move from the "natural" to the "unnatural". Prejudice and stereotype are the basis of much of the judicial decision making on lesbian and gay inequality as well. The absolute refusal to acknowledge lesbian and gay relationships, that is the sexual affectional relationships of lesbians and gays, permeates so many of these cases, particularly at the higher court levels. The fears, denial and stereotypes that shore up this refusal lie just barely below the surface in these decisions. The discomfort in dealing with these issues is so overpowering that it leads Justice Mahoney in *Egan* to make the following observation, "There are those, like theappellant, whose sexual orientation is a determining factor in their choice of partner."[8] How can the choice of heterosexuality be so invisible to a person deciding a case on gay rights? Similarly, what assumptions are at play that enable Justice Robertson to assert, with no apparent supporting evidence:

> Before us is a case in which a benefit has been conferred on a narrow class of persons who can be readily identified and who are in financial need because of a pattern of financial interdependency characteristic of heterosexual couples and which cannot in any reasonable way be deemed relevant to same-sex couples or, for that matter, other non-spousal relationships.[9]

I want to explore another aspect of the *Egan* case that also derives from the prejudices and stereotypes that form the foundation of the majority decisions in this case. The majority rejects Egan's claim because it was based on a similarly situated argument, that is the argument that gay couples are similarly situated to heterosexual couples and therefore should be granted the same spousal benefits, in this case pension benefits. This is a literal application of *Andrews* that defies logic. The issue is whether the applicants meet the equality test as established in *Andrews*. It is irrelevant whether or not they also meet the similarly situated test rejected by the Supreme Court of Canada. The rejection of a test does not transform the test to one of disentitlement.

However, despite the terrible problems with the *Egan* decision, I must say that I do take some perverse pleasure in it. I have been arguing for some time that lesbians and gays should not be pursuing the spousal benefit, "we're just like you" route, but should be joining with other oppressed groups whose definitions of family are not so spousally focused to challenge the use of spousal relationships as a vehicle through which benefits are channelled. Both of the majority judges advert to this issue in their pooling of so-called "same sex" couples with other non-spousal and non-sexual relationships, that is cohabiting "siblings, friends and relatives"[10]. In the context in which it is done, this renders lesbians and gays invisible as sexual and sexually active people. However, for me it confirms that the question — why privilege (hetero)sexual relationships? — is the right one. The majority judges include non-sexual relationships in order to point to the absurdity of the whole question of the extension of benefits. However, to me this is not only not absurd; it is the central question.

I have two more comments that I want to make about *Egan*. The first is that *Bliss*[11] is back. Unbelievable as it may seem, we are, yet again, going to have to deal with the circular logic of *Bliss*, that discrimination against a subset of an oppressed group is not discrimination against that group. In *Egan*, we have:

> When compared to the unit or group which benefits by the challenged law, the plaintiffs fall into the general group of non-spouses and do not benefit because of their non-spousal status ratherthan because of their sexual orientation.[12]

This would seem to be the flip side of *Bliss* because an oppressed group may be a subset of a larger group that may be experiencing the same treatment means that the oppressed group is not discriminated against by that treatment. This *Bliss*-type logic should have been dispelled by the Supreme Court of Canada's decision in *Janzen*[13] in which the Court held that the fact that man may be subjected to sexual harassment as well as women does not mean that sexual harassment is not a form of sex discrimination.

This is not an isolated incident. *Bliss* is back in *Rodriguez* when Justice Sopinka asks the question; "whether a claim by the terminally ill who cannot commit suicide without assistance can be supported on the ground that [the *Criminal Code* provision] discriminates against all disabled persons who are unable to commit suicide without assistance."[14] This is *Bliss* directly, This is serious bad news for equality jurisprudence.

The other comment that I wanted to make flowing from *Egan* is that it is truly surprising that there now seems to be a general consensus that sexual orientation is an analogous ground, but still the claims of lesbian and gays are being rejected. In *Mossop*[15], the claim should have been sexual orientation, not family status. In *Egan* it should have been marital status, not sexual orientation. Thus, the shell game goes on. This raises the difficult problem of compound discrimination and multiple grounds. The problems are complex and numerous. One has to fit one's experience(s) into the appropriate ground, that is pick the right shell or shells. One has to present one's experience(s) in terms of the shells in a way that does not allow one's experience(s) to fall through the spaces between the shells. At the same time, one wants to present one's experience(s) under the different equality headings so that they are seen as integrally related, as a compound whole, and not as separate (un)grounded parts.

In this regard, I was really happy to read the *Sparks*[16] decision that Martha Jackman discussed. In that case an African-Canadian single mother on social assistance challenged the reduced eviction notice requirements for public housing tenants and was found to have been discriminated against on the basis of race, sex and income. The Court didn't seem to be overwhelmed by the different grounds or feel obliged to pick the primary one or to reject them all. However, I was disappointed that the compound nature of these oppressions was not discussed. Did they see Irma Sparks as a whole person or was she for them simply her discriminated against parts?

I want to come back now to the post modern indeterminacy of equality. This indeterminacy means that, in post modern terms, challenges to authorship, to tradition, (that is in the legal context, precedent, traditional notions of legal reasoning and methodology, andobjectivity and neutrality) and to notions of subjectivity arise fairly immediately in the face of the overt kind of reading-in that equality requires. This is, I think, a good thing. The more that judges, legal academics and lawyers are required to take responsibility for the values reflected in their legal analysis, argument and decisions, the better. In raising these issues, there are lots of connections to the work and thinking of Bill Lederman as we heard this morning. There is very little to hide behind when applying an equality analysis, although certainly, in some of the cases you can see the judge desperately trying to do it. Some of the detailed and painful wranglings over the precise wording and application of *Andrews* seem more like attempts to hide behind or bury oneself in the words of *Andrews*, rather than put oneself, one's values,and one's decisions on the line.

In this, *Andrews* must be one of the most dissected, reconstructed, reformed, transformed, distorted, judgments ever. One result of this word-mongering is that equality is appropriately becoming subjected to the same critiques directed against post modernism, i.e., that it is elitist and inaccessible.

The judicial language of equality, like the language of post modernism, is becoming increasingly obscure and incomprehensible. Now, I do know that this is not a new critique with respect to judicial decisions, but it is rather paradoxical that the legal language of equality is becoming so inaccessible and so incomprehensible.

Of course, accessibility and equality are not just issues in terms of language. The point about who is bringing the s.15 *Charter* challenges has been made innumerable times, but I do feel the need to say it yet again. A quick review of recent *Charter* cases confirms that s.15 is largely being invoked by people of privilege. Most of the s.15 cases are being brought under analogous grounds. The openness in s.15 to analogous grounds is critically important. I agree with Madam Justice Wilson in *Andrews* that the *Charter* does not reflect, and we don't even know, all of the varied and complex bases on which we subject groups to inequalities. Of course the grounds are not immutable as they do and will shift and change over time. However, openness of the grounds encourages those with privilege to explore another potential route to shore up or to add to their privilege. By and large the courts seem to be doing a good job in rejecting these claims, thanks to the *Andrews/Turpin* test of group-based social, legal and political disadvantage. Nevertheless, it is disconcerting to see the numbers and types of these cases. As of yet, the negative decisions do not seem to be stemming the flood of these cases.

I recognize that human rights codes and the *Charter* have very different jurisdictions. However, despite these differences between the *Charter* and codes, it should give us pause to consider when one looks at who is bringing human rights complaints and who is bringing *Charter* challenges. There is something distinctly wrong with the *Charter* side of the picture, a wrongness that reflects additional layers of inequalities in terms of access and sense of entitlement.

I have referred to the *Andrews/Turpin* test for who fits within the grounds of discrimination and I am certainly one who argues that test should apply to enumerated, as well as non-enumerated grounds — that the requirement of pre-existing group disadvantage should apply with respect to gender and race for example, as well, and for the same reasons, that it would apply to any analogous ground. Having invoked the words of this test, which is a very important and appropriate test, I need to pause to make a critical comment about the term disadvantage upon which the test focuses and which has become one of the key words used to define inequality. This is a lesson that I learned from Patricia Monture. Professor Monture rejects the description of oppressed groups as disadvantaged:

> Generically I am speaking about racism and sexism and classism and all of the other isms and of how the individuals who fit those stereotypical classifications get qualified as disadvantaged. We are only disadvantaged if you are using a white, middle class yardstick....Disadvantage is a nice, soft comfortable word to describe dispossession, to describe a situation of force whereby our very existence, our histories, are erased continuously right before our eyes. Words like disadvantage conceal racism.[17]

The disadvantage is from the perspective of the dominant group. For the subordinated group it is oppression. Hester Lessard in her article on the decisions of Madam Justice Wilson raises a similar critique of disadvantage when she argues that, "we need to examine the cultural norms embedded in the concept of disadvantage which is increasingly presented as the bench mark of a social equality approach."[18] She asks who controls the definitions of advantaged and disadvantaged and questions the assumption that there is agreement on what it means to be these things. In asking this, she is raising the concern that the shift from the formal equality approach to what she describes as a social equality approach may be a shift in name only. The social equality model may also require a single and dominant notion of social prosperity which is equally, if more subtly, asssimilationist as the formal equality model. Professor Lessard is, with a different focus, asking the same question that many others have asked and continue to ask. It is an exceedingly important question: whether equality is trapped forever in a comparative, assimilationist model or is capable of breaking out of that model, bringing oppressed peoples with it.

Thus, my aside on disadvantage is the insight that perhaps we should not use the term to refer to oppressed groups and that we should be mindful at all times of the potential for equality to be used to mean and prescribe assimilation.

The post modern nature of equality means that the terrain on which it lies is constantly shifting and changing and that within and between decisions there are great inconsistencies. In so many judgments it seems to me that the differences between dissent and majority are vast and are worlds apart in terms of approach and analysis, as well as result. With respect to some cases, I find the divergences disturbing. In other cases the differences reflect the complexity and contradictions that so many of these issues present. This raises the inevitable question whether a legal forum, a place in which issues tend to be simplified and in which "answers" are required, is an appropriate places to "resolve" equality issues. My response to this issue is that there is no place in which it is **in**appropriate to address equality issues. What happens with equality in the courts affects how equality issues are raised, fought for and resisted in other forums. The reverse is also true in that what happens on the streets, in the class room, in the legislature, has an impact on what happens in the court room. There is no right or best place to advocate or adjudicate equality. It is being negotiated, contested, defined, adjudicated everywhere, all of the time.

The uncertainty of equality is not necessarily bad but it makes the equality project an exceedingly complex and amorphous one. For those of us who advocate for equality, there are seldom clear victories and there are certain losses, although the losses sometimes come with spectacular dissents. Equality is still very much in its post modern phase and there are very fewdefining features. David Lepofsky in a recent article[19] describes the judicial approach to equality rights as a fast moving accelerating roller coaster which took a dramatic plunge downward in 1990 with the Supreme Court of Canada decisions in *McKinney*[20], *Hess*[21], *R. v. S.*[22], but with *Keegstra*[23] providing a turn on the track and a glimmer of hope that the ascent will resume. He describes us as being at some kind of roller coaster crossroad, with the car dangling on the question as to wether we will reascend to the promising heights of *Andrews* and *Turpin*[24], leaving behind *McKinney* and *Hess* and *R. v. S.*, or whether we have started the downward path to excused inequality.

Much as I like the roller coaster image, it is too linear and uni-dimensional, even with all of its ups and downs and sharp turns, to describe the judicial approach to equality. The equality decisions are all over the place and even to discuss them in terms of trends or directions is to impose an order that just is not there. There are some small points of clarity, but by and large equality is truly a post modern term with no fixed meaning.

I want to point out another shared problem between equality and post modernism, one that relates to Patricia Monture's critique of disadvantage. In looking at this I refer to the work of some African American feminist scholars who have critiqued post modernism. I apply their critiques of post modernism to equality. Specifically I will borrow here from Patricia Hill Collins[25]. A problem with equality, as with post modernism itself, is the threat of de-politicization. Equality opens the door to recognition and discussion of "difference". However, without "attention to the role of power and domination in the construction of difference", the invocation of difference may be just an affirmation of the status quo or it may even involve descent into "unrestrained relativism". As with Hill Collins' critique of post modernism, equality has no clear and significant implication for practice. The *Andrews/Turpin* decisions did provide important tools that do address power and domination within the equality context, but the *Andrews/Turpin* test itself is somewhat post modern.

The equality project is to redress inequalities and to ensure that power and domination are always read into the equality analysis. In the words of Hester Lessard this is about, "confrontingand resisting practices of domination."[26] One of my concerns about our ability to see and address equality in terms of practices of domination is the reference to personal characteristics in *Andrews* that has been become a defining feature of the s.15 test of discrimination. The distinctions that create or reinforce the inequalities are described as based on personal characteristics, and it is said that "irrelevant personal differences" cannot justify differential treatment or result. This choice of words is very unfortunate. I would say that, in our extremely gendered and lesbian-hating society, nothing about my gender or my sexuality is irrelevant to me or to society. While both my gender and my sexuality are deeply personal, in the larger social context neither are personal at all, that is, they are not about me. I would describe neither my gender nor my sexual identity, nor any of their social manifestations, as characteristics. In this society, they are too important, too much defining of who I am, to be described simply as "characteristics". In order to move from personal characteristics to group-based claims, one has to read in the stereotype.[27] Conversely, as a member of the dominant group with respect, for example, to race and disability, I have tended to view my race and non-disabledness as irrelevant and as personal characteristics. In other words, I think this characterization of the foci of oppression as relating to "personal characteristics" comes from a position of dominance and privilege. The failure to incorporate notions of dominance into the definition depoliticizes the equality project. It becomes a project about mistakes and disadvantage rather than oppression.

I have one final issue that I want to raise with respect to the post modern complexity and uncertainty of equality. What I see happening in the face of this is that many courts, particularly lower courts, are refusing to deal with the s.15 arguments. They are simply dismissing them with little or no analysis or canvassing of the issues, or they are, simplistically and without comment, using discrimination to justify discrimination. There is no real exploration of the potential inequalities that may be there. I want to refer very briefly to three cases in this regard.

The first is *R. v. White*[28], a decision of the Nova Scotia County Court. This was a s.15 challenge to the anti-prostitution section of the *Criminal Code*, based on the disproportionate number of women, as compared to men charged, which was 5 to 1. Although the Court found that there were a disproportionate number of female prostitutes as compared to male prostitutes, this did not explain the imbalance in charges. The offence applies to customers, as well as to prostitutes and there was no evidence that the prohibited conduct was committed more often by prostitutes than by their customers. However, the Court held that the enforcement did not constitute discrimination based on sex. The reason was that the primary enforcement mechanism is through the use of decoys from the Halifax police force and there are very few women on that police force, there being 15 female police officers and 300 male police officers. In addition, it is dangerous and difficult work for a female decoy. Those dangers and difficulties which include, "aggressive competitors, pimps who are seeking new workers and protecting territories,intoxication and a threat of physical harm"[29], are the working conditions of prostitutes. Surely in the context of a sex discrimination challenge, these sex-based oppressive working conditions at least deserve some further comment. Inequality justified by inequality does not equality promote.

The second case is *A.L. v Saskatchewan Crimes Compensation Board*[30]. This was a challenge to the "reasonably prudent person" test applied to an abused woman pursuant to the legislation. In this case, the test resulted in a reduction in the award to the applicant because she continued to cohabit with her abuser and because she should have been aware that her actions on the date in question would aggravate him and lead to his violent behaviour. The Women's Legal and Education Action Fund (LEAF) intervened but was only allowed to present written submissions which Justice Gerwing assured us that they had read. With no discussion of the issues, the court found that the reasonably prudent test was sufficiently nuanced to take into account the battered spouse syndrome. Who could have read a LEAF brief on this subject, or for that matter the decision in *Lavallee*[31], and refer, without comment, to the battered *spouse* syndrome? This is formal equality at its most blatant.

The final case that I want to refer to is *R. v. Willocks*[32]. This was a challenge to the alternative justice programs operated by aboriginal communities in Ontario. The challenge was an attempt by the plaintiff to gain access to a diversionary program. Justice Vaillancourt discussed all the diversion programs in operation in Ontario and then made his finding that these programs are not based on enumerated grounds or personal characteristics attributed to individuals on the basis of their association with a group identified with those grounds. If programs were so based, the aboriginal programs specifically were protected under s. 15(2) on the basis that an affirmative action program need not be designed to address all groups suffering similar disadvantage and on the basis that it is permissible to establish priorities. While I am not sure what I think should or could have been done in this case, I think there are serious problems with the limited s.15 analysis that is given, as well as with the pro forma application of s.15(2). However, the specific thing that I want to point out is that it is not until the twelfth page of a 13 page decision that we are told that the applicant is Jamaican Canadian. We discover this only in the context of the statement that, "the communities with which the applicant identifies himself (Canada's black community or black Jamaican Canadian community) are not precluded from making proposals to operate similar projects suited to their own needs and resources." A last minute passing reference to race does not seem like an equality analysis to me.

I fear a judicial reversion to a *Canadian Bill of Rights* type approach to s.15, that is a dismissal of, or refusal to engage with, the issues of inequality. I think there are serious problems with section 15. In keeping with my post modern theme, I do not think these problems lead to a determination that s.15 is either a good thing or a bad thing, harmful or helpful. It simply is. We work with it, to shape and direct it, and use it to confront and challenge the practices of domination.

When I am feeling overwhelmed by this, I go and reread some of the equality decisions that have confronted practices of domination, or I go and read the list of authorities relied upon in the *Mossop* decision, for example. There I read the names of Audre Lorde, Jewelle Gomez, Adrienne Rich, Patricia Williams, all of whose work was referred to in the dissenting judgment of Madam Justice L'Hereux-Dube, and I think — YES! These and other equality activists, writers, and critical thinkers have become part of the legal equality analysis in Canada at the level of our highest court. Those who want to participate in this project will have to read, think about, and discuss the work of people like Audre Lorde and Patricia Williams. This to me is exciting and gives me hope for change. To me these authors are what s.15 should be, can be, and is all about.

NOTES

1. *Egan et al. v. The Queen* (1993), 103 D.L.R. (4th) 336 at p.359
2. *Rodriguez v. A.G. of Canada*, [1993] 3 S.C.R. 519 at p. 616. McLaughlin is quoting from *R. V. Swain*, [1991] 1 S.C.R. 933 at 992 per Lamer C.J.
3. Simone de Beauvoir, *The Ethics of Ambiguity* (New Jersey: Citadel, 1948) p.83
4. *McKinney v. University of Guelph*, [1990] 3 S.C.R. 229
5. *Rosen v. The Queen*, [1992] T.C.J. No. 699 (Tax Court of Canada)
6. *Andrews v. Law Society of British Columbia*, [1989] 1 S.C.R. 143
7. *Lister and Lister v. The Queen*, [1992] T. C. J., No. 674 (Tax Court of Canada)
8. *Supra*, n.1 at p.342
9. *Ibid* at p. 400
10. *Ibid* at p. 395
11. *Bliss v. Attorney-General of Canada*, [1979] 1 S.C.R. 183 (overruled by *Brooks v. Canada Safeway Ltd.*, [1989] 1 S.C.R. 1219). This is the case in which the Supreme Court of Canada held that discrimination against pregnant "people" is not sex discrimination because not all women are pregnant.
12. *Supra*, note 1 at p.343
13. *Janzen v. Pharos Restaurant*, [1989] S.C.R. 1252
14. *Supra*, note 2 at p. 612
15. *Mossop v. Attorney General of Canada*, [1993] 1 S.C.R. 554
16. *Dartmouth-Halifax County regional Housing Authority v. Sparks* (1992), 12 N.S.R. (2d) 389 (Co. Ct.)
17. Patricia Monture, "Ka-Nin-Geh-Heh-Gah-E-Sa-Nonh-Yah-Gah", (1986) 2 C.J.W.L. 159 at p.161
18. Hester lessard, "Equality and Access to Justice in the Work of Bertha Wilson", (19) 15 Dalhousie L.J. 35 at p. 59
19. David Lepofsky, "The Canadian Judicial approach to Equality Rights: Freedom Ride or Rollercoaster?" (1992) 1 N.J.C.L. 315
20. *Supra* note 4
21. *R. v. Nguyen,* (sub nom. *R. v. Hess*), [1990] 2 S.C.R. 906
22. *R. v. S.(S.)*, [1990] 2 S.C.R. 254
23. *R. v. Keegstra*, [1990] 3. S.C.R. 697
24. *R. v. Turpin*, [1989] 1 S.C.R. 1296
25. "The State of the Art", (1991) Vol.VIII No.5 *The Women's Review of Books* 22
26. *Supra* note 18
27. I get this notion of reading in the stereotype from Patricia Williams, "The Death of the Profane" in *The Alchemy of Race and Rights* (Cambridge, Mass.; Harvard University Press, 1991).
28. *R. v. White* (1992), 118 N.S.R. (2d) 414 (Co. Ct.) at p. 416
29. *Ibid*
30. *A.L. v. Saskatchewan Crimes Compensation Board*, [1992] 6 W.W.R. 577 (Sask. C.A.) at p. 583
31. *R. v. Lavallee*, [1990] 1 S.C.R. 852
32. *R. v. Willocks* (1993), 14 C.R.R. 373 (Ont. Court P.D.)

Rodriguez and Equality Rights

Lynn Smith

It is a great pleasure to be here and to take part in this Symposium. I know that Professor Lederman's primary interest was not in the field of equality rights but I did discover that he wrote a case comment on *The Queen v. Drybones*[1] in 1970, reprinted in *Continuing Canadian Constitutional Dilemmas*[2]. Professor Lederman wrote about *Drybones* as follows:

> We seem to have here the formula for a very effective blending of judicial and parliamentary powers, a formula that stimulates appropriate judicial activism in favour of the specified rights and freedom of the citizen, and yet still gives the last word to an ordinary majority in the democratically elected Parliament of Canada.[3]

With hindsight, the celebration of achievement under the *Canadian Bill of Rights* could not have been more inappropriate. *Drybones* proved to be virtually the only successful example of a claim under the *Canadian Bill of Rights*[4]. Even the limited scope that it provided for striking down legislation proved too terrifying for the courts. We could speculate about whether, in about five or eight years, we will be saying the same thing about the *Charter* equality rights. However, that is not my major theme today. I do not choose to be as pessimistic as perhaps one could be about the state of affairs under section 15. I will focus on the *Rodriguez*[5] decision in the Supreme Court of Canada and on one particular aspect of the case: its treatment of the adverse impact discrimination argument.

A few years ago, when the *Andrews*[6] case was argued in the Supreme Court of Canada, the Women's Legal Education and Action Fund (LEAF) and various other public interest organizations intervened because this was the first *Charter* equality rights case to reach that court. The issue in *Andrews* was the constitutionality of a citizenship requirement for the practice of law in British Columbia and it was not obvious that this was the kind of case in which LEAF and the other public interest intervenors would seek to become involved. However, recognizing the indeterminacy of the equality rights provisions and the importance of attempting to shape the ensuing discourse, LEAF and the other intervenor groups concentrated on trying to achieve a substantive definition of equality that would have an impact on members of disadvantaged groups. This was seen as preferable to a definition of equality that would have been of a more abstract and generic nature. In the outcome, *Andrews* can be seen as representing quite a dramatic departure from the previous existing model for equality rights, found in the United States jurisprudence. There are two related ways in which this was so.

The first was the limitation that the court imposed in *Andrews*: denial of access to equality rights protection outside claims involving a disadvantaged group invoked by the list in section 15, or analogous claims. Thus, there was a limitation to preclude claims by, for example, one commercial enterprise on the basis that it was unhappy with a form of regulation that affected it and not its competitor. The second was the simultaneous opening of access to section 15 claims based on adverse impact or unintended discrimination. Contrary to the position under the equal protection clause in the Fourteenth Amendment to the United States Constitution, where some intention to discriminate on the part of the state must be found, the Supreme Court in *Andrews* indicated that adverse impact claims (that is, based upon situations where the Government has not expressly, or intentionally, put a discriminatory provision into the legislation or practice, but where the impact on a particular group is nevertheless discriminatory) would be allowed. This was an important conclusion, and in effect it reflected a trade-off, based upon an assessment that if there were to be an equality rights provision in Canada that extended to adverse impact claims it would not be possible, at the same time, to allow for an unlimited range of claims, based upon any ground whatsoever[7]. Extension to adverse impact claims with no limitation as to grounds would likely result in a wholly ineffective equality rights section since the courts would soon aim to interpret it so as to permit, for example, government regulation of industry and a progressive tax system. To use a metaphor, the trade-off would seek to achieve a narrow and focused beam, as opposed to a very pale and diffused light. In *Andrews*, and then in some subsequent cases such as *Turpin*[8] and *Brooks v. Canada Safeway*[9], we do see significant adherence to a substantive notion of equality[10], arguably made possible by the trade-off described above.

After reviewing some of the aspects of the framework that the courts developed for analyzing equality claims, I will discuss the use of it in the *Rodriguez* case. The framework begins with *Andrews*, *Turpin* and *Reference re: Workers' Compensation Act*[11], but a later significant case which summarizes it is *R. v. Swain*[12]. The issue there was the treatment of persons found "not guilty by reason of insanity" and thus the enumerated ground of mental disability.

The courts said there has to be a three-stage inquiry under section 15. First, it must be determined whether there is a denial of equality before or under the law, or equal protection or benefit of the law. Second, if there is a denial of equality, it must be determined if there is discrimination. That is where the issue of the ground comes in: is it a case based upon either an enumerated or analogous ground? A second prong to that second stage is whether the definition of discrimination set out in *Andrews*[13] is met. Third, if there is a denial of equality with discrimination, it must be determined if it passes section 1; does it constitute a reasonable limit prescribed by law and demonstrably justifiable in a free and democratic society?

As mentioned earlier, a key pillar in the analysis is that only claims involving the so-called personal characteristics named in section 15 — race, colour, national or ethnic origin, religion, sex, mental or physical disability and age — or analogous ones, fall within the purview of section 15, and others are excluded. Another pillar is that section 15 gives the right to equality not only with respect to express differentiation, but also to unintended discriminatory effect. Finally, there is some significant authority now as to the implications of the statement in *Andrews* that identical treatment may not amount to equal treatment:

> It must be recognized at once, however, that every difference in treatment between individuals under the law will not necessarily result in equality and, as well, that identical treatment may frequently produce serious inequality.[14]

The *Weatherall*[15] case, involving searches by female prison guards, is an example of a specific application of this principle:

> The affirmative action program justified under s.15(2), which has enabled female officers to work at Collins Bay even though male guards are not employed in the living areas of the women's Prison at Kingston, justifies, by virtue of the opening words of s.15(2), any intrusion on the equality rights of male inmates under s.15(1) which are reasonably necessary to make that program work.[16]

Looking at that framework, and asking how much impact does it and the *Andrews* case continue to have, I am going to make just four comments, followed by a detailed discussion of the fourth.

First, it is not yet clear how the Supreme Court will deal with claims where there are enumerated grounds but no particular evidence of disadvantage, for example, claims under the equality provision by men, in contexts where men are not socially or politically disadvantaged in a relevant way. Madam Justice Wilson referred to this issue in *McKinney*[17], which dealt with mandatory retirement in universities. Justice Wilson questioned whether it would be necessary, even with a claim under an enumerated ground, to show some disadvantage independent of the legislation that is at issue. On the other hand, the Supreme Court in *Hess*[18] signalled that it was not particularly attracted to this type of asymmetrical approach. The Federal Court of Appeal decision in *Schachtschneider*[19] provides a contrary indication more consistent with the dicta in *McKinney*. It involved the income tax provision that disadvantaged married people in comparison with those living common law with respect to dependents' deductions. The Court in *Schachtschneider*, considering whether married people could claim under section 15 on the basis of marital status, concluded that the Court should look at the factors that the Supreme Court suggested in *Turpin* to see whether there was political or social disadvantage, or historical stereotyping. Since married people have historically, and in most contexts, been advantaged compared with the rest, the fact that in some instances unmarried women have been disadvantaged was irrelevant. Section 15 analysis is not a question of simply adding new generic grounds, but of assessing the specific claim in its context.

A second, very important issue is what happens at the section 1 stage. Some members of the Supreme Court are inclined to apply a different and more lenient test when a violation is found under section 15 than when it is found under other provisions of the *Charter*, for example under a legal rights provision. I think there is evidence in *Rodriguez* that the highly forgiving approach to section 1 analysis is winning out.

Third, there is a hint in the *Schachter*[20] case, which involved the distinction between parents who gave birth to their children and those who adopt, that it is not going to be overly easy to obtain inclusion as an analogous ground: the Chief Justice expressed concern that the Crown had conceded that the distinction between adoptive and birth parent was one that fell within section 15[21].

Fourth, and this is where I will spend more time, there appears to be a real division in the Supreme Court over the true extent to which unintended effects will be included within the scope of discrimination. Permit me to review the history of this. In *Andrews*[22] there were *dicta* stating that unintended discrimination is encompassed by section 15, adopting the approach in *Ontario Human Rights Commission v. Simpson Sears (O'Malley)*[23]. This statement was repeated in a few subsequent cases, such as *McKinney* and *Tétreault-Gadoury*[24]. However, the Court in those cases was using the terms in a novel way, indeed, inconsistently with the way members of the Court used the terms in the *O'Malley* case. For example, *McKinney*, which was the mandatory retirement case, did not involve, on the face of it, a neutral rule that incidentally happened to have an impact on people over the age of 65. The mandatory retirement policy was straight-forward, express and intentional. Nevertheless, the Court referred to the conclusion that the *Charter* protects against adverse impact discrimination, which it said was at issue in *McKinney*[25]. The Court saw it the same way in *Tétreault-Gadoury*, which was another case involving an express and intentional provision based on age.

The Court's statements about adverse impact discrimination no doubt stemmed from the fact that the mandatory retirement provisions were viewed as aimed at assisting young people (to get into the employment market) rather than at harming those over 65. Nevertheless, I think it would be better if the terminology of unintentional or adverse impact discrimination were saved for cases such as *Sparks*[26]. There, the issue was the differential treatment of public housing tenants with respect to notice of eviction, compared with tenants in privately owned housing. The defence in *Sparks* conceded that women, blacks and social assistance recipients form a disproportionately large percentage of the tenants in public housing and, at one point, the NovaScotia Court of Appeal clearly treated this as an adverse impact discrimination case[27]. At another point, however, the Court said no, this was not an adverse impact analysis[28]. In my view, it is virtually a textbook case of a neutral rule that has an impact on particular groups in a manner that may be discriminatory, regardless of lack of intention.

Thus, looking at the cases up to *Rodriguez*, I think it is fair to say that the courts have been struggling with the meaning and application of the innovative notion that a constitutional guarantee of equality rights can apply to indirect and unintentional discrimination. *Rodriguez* is the first case to reach the Supreme Court in which a true adverse impact issue has arisen in an equality rights context. Of course, in freedom of religion cases effects-based analysis is commonplace. Beginning in *Edwards Books*[29], the Court has become well accustomed to looking at the effects of legislation rather than simply at its express terms.

Turning to *Rodriguez*, I think the Chief Justice must have written first although he did not, in the end, attract a majority. His recital of the facts is as follows:

> The facts of this case are straightforward and well known. Sue Rodriguez is a 42-year-old woman living in British Columbia. She is married and the mother of an 8 - year-old son. Ms. Rodriguez suffers from amyotrophic lateral sclerosis (ALS), whiah is widely known as Lou Gehrig's Disease; her life expectancy is between 2 and 14 months but her condition is rapidly deteriorating. Very soon she will lose the ability to swallow, speak, walk and move her body without assistance. Thereafter she will lose the capacity to breathe without a respirator, to eat without a gastrotomy and will eventually be confined to a bed.
>
> Ms. Rodriguez knows of her condition, the trajectory of her illness and the inevitability of how her life will end; her wish is to control the circumstances, timing and manner of her death. She does not wish to die so long as she still has the capacity to enjoy life. However, by the time she no longer is able to enjoy life, she will be physically unable to terminate her life without assistance.[30]

Ms. Rodriguez sought an order that would permit assistance in her suicide from a qualified medical practitioner. As we know, the majority of the court dismissed her claim under the three *Charter* sections that were cited: sections 7, 12 and 15. The majority consisted of Justices Sopinka, LaForest, Gonthier, Iacobucci and

Major. There were two dissents. One set of dissenting reasons by Madam Justice McLachlin found that there was a section 7 infringement, that the infringement was not justified under section 1 and that there should be the kind of remedy proposed by Chief Justice Lamer[31]. Chief Justice Lamer, with whom Justice Cory agreed (though Justice Cory also agreed with the other dissenters) found that there was an infringement of section 15(1) based upon the fact that section 241(b) of the *Criminal Code* prevents persons physically unable to end their own lives from choosing suicide while that option is open to other persons. Since physical disability is a listed ground in section 15, and persons with disabilities are the subject of unfavourable treatment in Canadian society, an adverse impact analysis led to the conclusion that there was a violation. Indeed, the Chief Justice said, in order "...to promote the objective of a more equal society, s.15(1) acts as a bar to the executive enacting provisions without taking into account their possible impact on already disadvantaged classes of persons."[32] After concluding that there was a violation, he went on to apply a pretty straightforward *Oakes*[33] type of analysis at the section 1 stage. The Chief Justice recognized an interesting and important feature of this case which is sometimes called the "dignity of risk" issue. He saw the purpose for the impugned legislation as protection for vulnerable people from helpful suggestions that they commit suicide, or from offers to assist them in doing so, but he asked why, in protectingvulnerable people, we should assume that physically disabled people are particularly vulnerable?[34] Ms. Rodriguez, for example, clearly had all of her mental faculties and apparently a strong will. Should we not assume that the *Criminal Code* will protect vulnerable people without an absolute bar against suicide by those who happen to be disabled? To assume otherwise may be to operate on the basis of a harmful stereotype with respect to people with disabilities.

Rodriguez resulted in a five to four decision with the majority dismissing the *Charter* claim and, implicitly, the analysis of adverse impact discrimination employed by the Chief Justice. Indeed, only one other judge agreed with him about that aspect. Justice Sopinka assumed there was a section 15 violation but said it was justified under section 1 in any event. In passing, he asked some questions about section 15 which may not bode well for its interpretation in future cases. For example, he asked whether there could be a section 15 violation based on physical disability when the claim was by someone terminally ill[35], given that all disabled persons are not terminally ill. I think that Chief Justice Lamer disposed of that question correctly when he pointed out that in the *Brooks*[36] case the Supreme Court decided that it did not matter that not all women are pregnant at one time; discrimination against pregnant women is still discrimination against women. Just as all pregnant women are women, all terminally ill persons unable to commit suicide without assistance are physically disabled.

In the other dissent, Madam Justice McLachlin and Madam Justice L'Heureux-Dubé state that *Rodriguez* was not a section 15 case at all, although it is unclear exactly why not. They state:

> ... this is not at base a case about discrimination under s.15 of the *Canadian Charter of Rights and Freedoms*, and that to treat it as such may deflect the equality jurisprudence from the true focus of s.15 [which is] to remedy or prevent discrimination against groups subject to stereotyping, historical disadvantage and political and social prejudices in Canadian society.[37]

Instead, they see the case as being about arbitrariness and should be properly viewed under section 7. They define the arbitrariness in terms of the inequality that is created when able-bodied persons are able to make choices about ending their own lives that persons with physical disabilities are not.

It is unclear to me why the arbitrariness concept and section 7 were preferable to a straightforward discussion of equality. One possibility is that these judges felt there could be a more rigorous section 1 analysis when there was a "liberty or security of the person" violation than when the violation was under section 15.

My conclusion then, is that this is a difficult issue for the courts. Despite the number of times that the Supreme Court has stated that adverse impact discrimination comes under section 15 of the *Charter*, in the first true test of the application of the concept we see a substantial majority of the Court rejecting the argument. I do not want to use an analogy that suggests something natural and inevitable about it, but I think the approach to equality the Supreme Court took in *Andrews* was, in some ways, very new, like the opening of a new channel for a river. There will be a tendency to move back into the course that was long established. A few more years will tell us how pronounced that tendency is in the case of *Charter* equality rights.

NOTES

1. *R. v. Drybones,* [1970] S.C.R. 282.
2. W.R. Lederman, "A Comment on the Canadian Bill of Rights and the Judgment of the Supreme Court of Canada in the case of: The Queen v. Drybones (1970)" in *Continuing Canadian Constitutional Dilemmas: Essays on the Constitutional History, Public Law and Federal System of Canada* (Toronto: Butterworths, 1981) chapter 25 at 415-418.
3. *Ibid* at 418.
4. Until the *Canadian Charter of Rights and Freedoms* somehow breathed tiny sparks of new life into it: see *R. v. Hayden,* [1993] 6 W.W.R. 655 (Man. C.A.) and *Singh et al. v. Minister of Employment and Immigration,* [1985] S.C.R. 177.
5. *Rodriguez v. British Columbia (Attorney General),* [1993] 3 S.C.R. 519.
6. *Andrews v. Law Society of British Columbia,* [1989] 1 S.C.R. 143.

7. See W. Black and L. Smith "The Equality Rights" in Beaudoin, G.A., Ratushny, E. (eds.), *The Canadian Charter of Rights and Freedoms* (2d ed.), Carswell, Toronto, 1989, 557-651.

8. *R. v. Turpin*, [1989] 1 S.C.R. 1296.

9. *Brooks v. Canada Safeway Ltd.*, [1989] 1 S.C.R. 1219.

10. By that I mean one which compares the situations of, for example, women and men, or racialized minorities and the majority in terms of their actual conditions (economic, social, political) rather than in terms of the written laws (often called "formal equality").

11. *Reference re: Workers' Compensation Act, 1983 (Nfld.), ss. 32, 34* (1989), 56 D.L.R. (4th) 765 (SCC).

12. *R. v. Swain*, [1991] 1 S.C.R. 933.

13. *Supra*, note 6 at 174-76; and *supra*, note 5 at 545-46.

14. *Supra*, note 6 at 143; and *supra*, note 5 at 545.

15. *Weatherall v. Canada (Attorney General)* (1988), 65 C.R. (3d) 27 (FCA).

16. *Weatherall v. Canada (Attorney General)* (1987), 59 C.R. (3d) 247 (FCTD) at 286; affirmed *supra*, note 16.

17. *McKinney v. University of Guelph*, [1990] 3 S.C.R. 229 at 392-93.

18. *R. v. Hess; R. v. Nguyen*, [1990] 6 W.W.R. 289.

19. *Schachtschneider v. R.*, [1994] 1 F.C. 40.

20. *Schachter v. Canada*, [1992] 2 S.C.R. 679.

21. *Ibid* at 695-96 and 721-22.

22. *Supra*, note 6 at 173.

23. *Ontario (Human Rights Commission) v. Simpson Sears Ltd.*, [1985] 2 S.C.R. 536.

24. *Tétreault-Gadoury v. Canada (Employment and Immigration Commission)*, [1991] 2 S.C.R. 22.

25. *Supra*, note 18 at 279.

26. *Dartmouth/Halifax County Regional Housing Authority v. Sparks* (1993), 101 D.L.R. (4th) 224 (N.S.C.A.).

27. *Ibid* at 228.

28. *Ibid* at 232.

29. *R. v. Edwards Books and Art Ltd.*, [1986] 2 S.C.R. 713.

30. *Ibid* at 530-31.

31. *Supra*, note 5 at 579, Chief Justice Lamer advocated a "personal remedy" in conjunction with a "constitutional exemption", incorporating many of the elements of the dissent of McEachern C.J.B.C. ([1993] 3 W.W.R. 553 at 576-77):

    (1) an application for a "constitutional exemption" must be made to a superior court;

    (2) the competency of the applicant must be certified in writing by a treating physician and an independent psychiatrist, and at least one of the physicians must be present when the applicant commits assisted suicide or the apparatus for such is operative;

    (3) also to be certified by the physicians is the physical inability of the applicant to commit suicide unassisted and the applicant's knowledge that (s)he has the continuing right to change her/his mind re the termination of her/his life;

    (4) 3 days notice must be given to the Regional Coroner before examination of the applicant by the psychiatrist, and the Regional Coroner (or physician nominee) may be present at the examination;

(5) the applicant must be examined daily by one of the certifying physicians to determine whether or not the applicant's intention remains unaltered and to confirm such for the Coroner if the suicide occurs;

(6) the "constitutional exemption" will expire in 31 days at which time all arrangements must be made inoperative; and

(7) the act causing the death of the applicant must be that of the applicant.

32. *Ibid* at 549.
33. *R. v. Oakes,* [1986] 1 S.C.R. 103.
34. *Supra*, note 5 at 562.
35. *Ibid* at 612.
36. *Supra*, note 10 at 1247; and *supra*, note 5 at 557.
37. *Ibid* at 616.

Part Four

FREEDOM OF EXPRESSION

Regulating Freedom of Expression the Canadian Way

Wayne MacKay

I am honoured to be a part of this symposium, both because I had the good fortune of knowing Professor Lederman personally, and because he spent his formative years at the Dalhousie Law School before emigrating to Queen's Faculty of Law.

There are very few areas of constitutional law that Professor Lederman has not written about, but one that he has not specifically addressed, at least as far as I could determine, is freedom of expression. In some ways that is not so surprising because, as Irwin Cotler points out,[1] in the first three years after the *Charter* we had more freedom of expression cases than we had in the previous one hundred and fifteen. Professor Lederman did, however, have clear ideas on the issue, and these were expressed as side comments in other articles, most coming from *Continuing Canadian Constitutional Dilemmas*.

A PRE-CHARTER PILLAR OF OUR CONSTITUTION

Professor Lederman, to no one's surprise, saw freedom of expression as a part of what we inherited from the phrase in the preamble to our *Constitution Act, 1867*, a constitution "similar in Principle to that of the United Kingdom." In that regard he quoted with clear approval Sir Arthur Goodhart's statement in the *Hamlyn Lectures* of 1952 as to the four pillars of the English constitution: the rule of law, representative government, freedom of speech, thought and assembly, and the independence of judges. It is interesting that everything being talked about at this symposium could be fitted into those four categories. Given this context one sees that freedom of expression was a very vital part of the Constitution, even prior to the *Charter*.

An implication of that, which is made evident in *Dolphin Delivery*[2] and other freedom of expression cases, is that political speech is particularly valuable. As Kathleen Mahoney pointed out in her presentation to this symposium, what is at the centre of legal protection of speech is clearly not what most would hold most central.

BALANCING DEMOCRACY AND INDEPENDENT COURTS

A second element of Professor Lederman's scholarship emphasizes the need to balance the respective roles of democratic legislatures and independent courts in a free and democratic society. We had some interesting debate this morning on that issue in relation to section 96 of the *Constitution Act, 1867*. In fact, drawing the line between the proper roles of independent courts and democratic legislatures is a critical question for speech as well.

In later years that kind of analysis was brought by Professor Lederman to the *Charter*. This may explain why his writing on the *Charter* was more focused on its section 1 and "reasonable limits" on rights in a free and democratic society than on substantive freedoms. It remains a crucial type of analysis. Most of the difficult speech analysis in Canada has been resolved by a balancing of interests in section 1. There is an implicit, if not explicit, recognition that drawing the line between courts' and legislators' roles is essential. For example, assessing the role of the legislature in enacting laws to protect the public from hate propaganda or obscenity and assessing the role of the courts in second guessing those kinds of legislative decisions is presently controversial yet fundamental.

Professor Lederman indicated on a number of occasions that legislatures and courts should be partners, not rivals. This type of thinking provides a positive basis for this crucial separation between law drafters and judicial interpreters. If they are to be seen as essentially co-operative partners, then the courts' proper role may include interpretation that adds power to laws that promote the values inherent in the Constitution. Lederman never goes so far as to advocate the pro-active decision-making I would like to see. However, his version of the division between legislatures and the courts cannot simply be seen as elaborate gamesmanship. Rather, the "partners, not rivals" view sets the stage for greater contextual and pro-active interpretation by the judiciary.

RIGHTS VS. FREEDOMS

A third element which characterizes his view of freedom of expression is his emphasis on the differences between "rights" (such as those to vote, to a fair trial or to receive minority language education) and "freedoms" (such as freedom of expression). This was articulated in a 1986 article in the *Queen's Law Journal* and then repeated in *Constitutional Dilemmas*. He draws a clear line, at least in theory, between rights and freedoms. In fact, in Chapter 24 of *Constituional Dilemmas*, he returns to these distinctions by extensive citation of the 1969 *McRuer Report on Civil Rights*, parts of which he co-authored. That's interesting and perhaps telling in relation to where Lederman is coming from, at least initially, on freedom of expression. I will quote from that chapter to give you some idea of his views on this:

> The concept of liberties or freedoms in a duly precise scheme of legal terminology is the concept of option and opportunity for human activity that are residual in nature. These areas of conduct are free of specific legal regulation. In them the individual is free to act or do nothing without legal direction ... what is not forbidden is permitted.[3]

That's a very important sort of articulation, a classic liberal view on freedom of expression: there's the regulated area and the unregulated area and freedom of expression is largely residual. Whatever has not been regulated should be free.

He then goes on to recognize the potential breadth of freedom of speech and freedom of expression, obviously seeing this unregulated area as quite large: "It is potentially as various, far-reaching and unpredictable as the capacity of the human mind."[4] He continues, "Freedom of expression is the residual area of natural liberty remaining after the makers of the common law and the statute law have encroached upon it ..."[5] He also recognizes, then, not just statutory limitations but also common law and judicial limitations.

There are two parts to this analysis. He is obviously recognizing the potential breadth of freedom of expression, and in that sense he conforms to the classic liberal formulation of freedom of speech. It's extremely important that he's also noting, without flinching, regulations and limitations on freedom of expression, which is certainly not the American style.

His approach, of identifying what are the regulated and unregulated areas, is reflected in the decision in *Dolphin Delivery*. It was in this case that the Supreme Court of Canada first addressed these freedom of expression issues in the *Charter* context. The Court adopted his approach of identifying unregulated areas and then went on, in what has become a pattern in the Supreme Court of Canada, to balance the values under section 1. So, once you define the regulated area, its purposes and its effects, and once you define the unregulated area and the nature of the expression, then the real action in terms of making difficult choices comes under section 1.

While that by no means was original or solely attributable to Lederman, that certainly was part of his approach as well as the Court's. He emphasizes this view: "a liberal and democratic society needs enough law, but not too much law, and ... keeping this balance is always a delicate and difficult task."[6]

You can see recognized in the title to this talk, "Regulating Free Expression the Canadian Way", that the Americans have a very different approach to regulation of free expression. Such regulation is not an odd or outrageous concept in Canada. It is to some extent in the United States where the First Amendment is first in more than a numerical sense. This goes to the essence of how they define individual rights.

Lederman implicitly assumes that government intervention through the *Charter* would be negatively pre-emptive rather than pro-active in nature. This is close to the classic American judicial view of the role of their Constitution as negatively limiting governmental action, rather than being a tool for actively furthering the values enshrined in that document. Having taken the view that intervention through the *Charter* has a limiting character, he lays the foundation for all the jurisprudence developed later, for better and for worse.

Much of Lederman's view is reflected in what the Supreme Court of Canada has done in freedom of expression cases. One of the most disappointing aspects of this is that they see government participation as a largely negative activity. No pro-active interventions in the marketplace of speech to actually create freedom of expression are made. That's one of the dangers of drawing the line between rights which require pro-active interventions, such as the right to vote where we actually have to spend money so people can go out and vote, and other kinds of freedoms where the government doesn't have to pro-actively do anything. Lederman, though, seemed comfortable with this distinction.

ABSTRACT FREEDOMS AND PRACTICAL EQUALITY

A fourth element in Lederman's writing with respect to freedom of speech is the relationship of abstract freedoms to practical equality. Lederman starts with a fairly generous abstract view of the importance of freedom of expression, which is once again picked up in the early Supreme Court cases. This is linked to the first element I described: freedom of speech as one of the pillars of the English constitution, obviously valued as an important abstraction. However, having said that, Lederman goes on to recognize that those abstract values can be limited. By forsaking American absolutism in free speech and accepting the regulation of speech as the norm, he helped set the stage for the balancing of freedom of speech and equality.

In later Supreme Court cases, such as *Keegstra* and *Butler*, and even in other less obvious cases like *Slaight Communications* in the context of employer/employee relations, the Court recognized that you don't simply take an abstract concept and apply it, you must put it in the context of equality. I should point out that in Lederman's writings, both generally and in the *McRuer Report*, equality values were not the particular values that he was identifying. He was identifying values more traditionally connected with the democratic structure as the ones that should be limiting free expression. By updating that concept, you could now say that equality values would also be part of that democratic structure. I'll provide a few quotes to support this outrageous theory:

> Accordingly, the dilemma of justice for legislators and judges is to determine when equal treatment for all is the fair and proper thing, and when, on the other hand, some discriminations are necessary and fair.[7]

In other words, equality doesn't always require the same treatment; it may require different treatment. That concept allows the Supreme Court in cases like those involving obscenity and hate propaganda to argue that we don't have to treat all speech equally, that it is appropriate to discriminate among certain types of speech to exclude that which is degrading to vulnerable groups.

While Lederman did state his analysis at a highly abstract level, he accepted that these abstractions must be placed in a more concrete and particular context:

> Abstract general principles must be particularized by full and relevant detail in the laws, or they remain incomplete and ineffective in affording meaningful directions at the level of everyday affairs.[8]

He's arguing that in order to make an abstraction meaningful it does have to be put in context: it really doesn't have much meaning as a total abstraction. Lederman is looking at this limitation in terms of detail at the statutory level, but nonetheless that is on the way to the kind of contextual analysis that Madame Justice Wilson talks about in the *Edmonton Journal* case or that is applied to some extent in *Butler* and *Keegstra*. Having said this, for those of you who knew Professor Lederman and are aghast at the thought I may be suggesting that he was a feminist in disguise, I'm not (although maybe he was and that would provide for an interesting debate or discussion). I am certainly suggesting that he was not a total libertarian and in fact, he probably fell somewhere in between the two.

Lederman set the stage, I think, for the kind of contextual, feminist, pro-active decisions that Bertha Wilson wrote. Examine this quote from *Edmonton Journal*[9]:

> One virtue of the contextual approach ... is that it recognizes that a particular right or freedom may have a different value depending on the context. ... The contextual approach attempts to bring into sharp relief the aspect of the right or freedom which is truly at stake in the case as well as the relevant aspects of any values in competition with it. It seems to be more sensitive to the reality of the dilemma posed by the particular facts and therefore more conducive to finding a fair and just compromise between two competing values under s.1.

He laid the foundation largely by accepting that expression is something that could be regulated: yes, it is important; yes, it is part of the core of our democratic structure, but of course in a free and democratic society these things must be balanced, therefore, expression can be regulated for all kinds of legitimate purposes.

THE ANALYTICAL APPROACH OF THE SUPREME COURT

I would like to quickly take you through some of the major approaches that the Supreme Court has taken to interpreting freedom of expression. First, like so many things Canadian, the articulation of the Supreme Court's approach to freedom of expression can best be understood against an American backdrop: the whole American experience is so different in terms of how they view expression, and more particularly their intolerance for limitation on freedom of expression. This may explain as "Canadian", the difference in approach taken to hate propaganda and obscenity. However, what the Court does in those two cases, I would suggest, is exceptional to their general approach to defining freedom of expression in the *Charter* context, not the norm.

I would hold that while the Court maintains that they are not going to follow the United States, they are in fact doing so (which is a good Canadian tradition, of course). A lot of the terminology and concepts from United States jurisprudence have been adopted with very little critical examination of their underlying assumptions. Notwithstanding the differences between Canada and the United States which are often important in reaching different conclusions on matters such as obscenity and hate speech, there has been much adoption of American concepts. One good example is the Court's early pronouncements on the various rationales for the protection of freedom of expression under section 2(b).

David Lepofsky has done a very interesting critique of *Irwin Toy*[10] where he identifies nine different purposes for s.2(b) referred to by the Court, and these are mostly American in origin: securing democratic self-government, achieving good or intelligent government, fostering participation in political and social decision-making, providing a balance between stability and change in society, facilitating the search for truth and knowledge through a marketplace of ideas, promoting social pluralism and diversity, safeguarding individual autonomy and self-development, and providing the necessary underpinning for other rights and freedoms. The Court identifies these, yet still says we are different from the Americans in our freedom of expression but don't really explain what's behind the inclusion of some of those purposes and why we're different.

An Individualistic Focus on Rights

While ostensibly distancing themselves from the American tradition and adopting a more unique Canadian one, the Supreme Court is still very individualistic in their definition of free speech (although hate propaganda may be the exception). For example, in the *Dolphin Delivery* case, they directly recite the democratic, or so-called political instrumental theories, as justifying free speech in that context. In *Irwin Toy*, they get into the whole American debate about the free marketplace of ideas. At least some of the judges seem to adopt that approach almost uncritically. The American notion of a "free marketplace of ideas" as an instrument for truth-seeking and democracy has been subjected to a lot of criticism both in the American context and elsewhere.

One opportunity where the Court had a clear chance to distance themselves from the United States and really put a Canadian stamp on the issue was in *Ford v. A.G. Quebec*. The case concerned a language law in Quebec, and the court referred to the role of language in the process of collective self-actualization and autonomy. They went on at some length to examine theories that hold that in order to really express yourself and to maintain your identity you have to do it in your own language. Certainly parts of that opinion are close to an articulation of a Canadian variant of freedom of expression in the context of language. However, what the Court stopped short of doing was recognizing that they were really talking about protecting collective rights. The exercise of language rights exists primarily in a collective or group context (Francophones in Quebec, Anglophones outside Quebec) whereas the Court cast the debate much more in terms of the individual exercise of language rights. It seems that if they were really interested in distancing themselves from American individualistic analysis they would advocate a more communitarian approach, rather than utilizing American concepts such as the free marketplace of ideas without putting them into a Canadian context.

The Irwin Toy Test

I would like to briefly examine the test set forth in the *Irwin Toy* decision, since it constitutes a blueprint for the approach to freedom of expression under the *Charter*. The case sets out three basic tests in determining the question of *Charter* protection. The first part is: does the speech or activity actually fall within the scope of section 2(b)? Here, they ask two questions. First, does the speech have expressive content? One might have thought that, at some level, all speech has expressive content; presumably they mean something narrower. Second, a rather interesting but not much discussed exception is provided: violent speech which has a violent form. So they exclude non-expressive speech and violent speech, but everything else falls under s. 2(b).

The second stage after that initial exercise is to examine both the purposes and effects of the challenged legislation to see whether either violates the guarantee of free expression. Only after this step do they go on to the third part: to assess the values and functions behind freedom of expression, such as the pursuit of truth, self-actualization, political participation and so on.

Lepofsky in his sometimes unmerciful fashion takes on the Supreme Court and suggests that in fact they have gone too far, making determinations beyond the context of this case. Maybe one thing he's saying is that a commercial speech case may not have been the best opportunity to fully articulate the content of freedom of expression. Freedom of religion was articulated in the commercial context in *Big M Drug Mart*, however, so the use of a commercial speech case may not have been as accidental as it seems.

Connecting to Other Rights and Freedoms

One interesting element about the Supreme Court's approach to freedom of expression in early *Charter* cases is that they seem to understand their own decision in *Big M Drug Mart* to suggest that the rights should be viewed in the broader social context, and that *Charter* rights should also be put in the context of other rights within the document as a whole. It is important to note, however, that this balancing in context occurs at section 1. There doesn't seem to be much effort to put freedom of expression itself in the context of the rest of the *Charter*. How does it fit in with legal rights? How does it fit in with equality rights or with other categories of rights? These questions remain unaddressed.

There is little attempt to connect the various fundamental freedoms themselves. In equality and other areas the Court has gone to some length to try to fashion a comprehensive approach to the internal logic of a particular category of rights, and that hasn't happened with the fundamental freedoms. There's surprisingly little connection between approaches in freedom of religion, freedom of association, freedom of speech, and so forth. For example, it struck me that an analysis based on liberty would except violent speech from protection under section 2(b) of the *Charter* through a liberty-based definition of the fundamental freedoms. Alternatively, in light of the language in section 2(e), which protects peaceful assembly, it is worth noting that there is nothing in the language of free expression that limits it to peaceful expression. One approach would be to argue that since section 2(e) protects peaceful assembly and section 2(b) has no such limit, that violence could be in. What we have here is a package of fundamental freedoms, and you could argue that the language of section 2(e) or the paramountcy of liberty should colour an interpretation of section 2(b). We are left with no connections at all.

The Possibility of "Mutual Modification"

An improvement would be to make some connection between the various fundamental freedoms rather than looking at each in isolation, that there be a more genuinely "made in Canada" approach, and that we don't simply say that we're not following the American analysis but then continue in fact to use their concepts. This could arise from an application of Professor Lederman's "mutual modification" doctrine[11] (as drawn from the Privy Council's decision in *Parsons*) to the *Charter*. The uniquely Canadian dilemmas posed by powers granted under sections 91 and 92 of the 1867 *Constitution Act* include, for example, the co-existence of federal divorce powers with provincial control of the solemnization of marriage and the interrelation of property and civil rights powers of the provinces and the federal trade and commerce power. By "mutual modification" these powers are given meaning by contextualization within the document as a whole. One power is read not so broadly as to rob meaning from other related powers listed. For example, property and civil rights could swallow up trade and commerce, but the provincial power is not read so broadly as to vitiate the federal jurisdiction over trade and commerce.

Mutual modification can be brought to bear with similar common sense practicality in respect to *Charter* rights and in particular the fundamental freedoms. For example, before any section 1 balancing, there could be substantive limits placed on freedom of expression that prevent it from wiping out equality rights (as in the cases of hate literature and pornography) or other rights. This seems to be the Court's implicit approach on singling out violent speech as not protected; how can a government that is proscribed from taking away life, liberty or security of the person do so by protecting violent expression? This type of mutual modification should be made more explicit and comprehensive, thus saving the time and expense of proving exceptions under section 1.

Taking an Abstract Approach

I would also suggest that the Court has been abstract in its approaches to freedom of expression. In the equality area they have tried to be impact-oriented. When they apply section 1 and bring in equality values in expression cases like *Butler* and *Keegstra* they attempt to do this, but the general approach is to define freedom of expression in quite abstract terms. Both Lederman and the Supreme Court might well be accused of the classic "male" approach to the issue as opposed to a more contextualized analysis. In the actual articulation of rights the Court generally falls short.

This was the point emphasized by Justice Wilson, of course, in the *Edmonton Journal* case where she takes her colleagues to task for not properly contextualizing the interpretation of rights not just in section 1 but also in section 2(e). She argues that "a right or freedom may have different meanings in different contexts."[12]

One of the dangers of too abstract an approach is shown in the consequences of the *Butler* decision. The definition of valid censorship allows this decision to be used either as an attack on equality or to buttress equality values. There, they do take account of what affects women and children, evincing some concern for a contextualization of the harm analysis. Yet, it is left unclear whose community is to be consulted in order to contextualize analysis for particular types of literature: is it the general Canadian population, the readers at whom the literature is targeted, or the group who potentially is suffering dehumanization?

It's important to note that *Butler* has been predominately used to exclude gay and lesbian pornography from Canada. I think the reason for that impact is the very abstract concept of valid censorship which hasn't been considered in the context of different communities. We talk about community standards, but of course the question is, which community. Paul Wollaston's article[13], "When Will They Ever Get It Right? A Gay Analysis of *R. v. Butler*", discusses the heterosexist bias of the community standard test used in and after *Butler*. We have made it beyond the white male community to include women's perceptions of the impacts of pornography, but we haven't made it to looking at the gay and lesbian communities' perception of what's acceptable, or that of various visible minorities or aboriginals. We have a long way to go in contextualizing these kinds of things.

Grounding in Traditional Norms

Professor Elliot made the point at this symposium that one of the things that characterized Professor Lederman's approach to constitutional law was normative grounding; he didn't want to be descriptive, he wanted to base things in norms. I think that's a correct approach and very much to his credit. Having praised him, I would observe that those norms are in fact rather traditional norms. There is nothing wrong with that, but the kinds of constitutional norms he's identifying are the kinds that came out of that 1952 Hamlyn lecture. There are many other norms that have been articulated since, such as those that come out of the *Prostitution Reference*.

There, both Dickson and Wilson ground their decisions in constitutional norms, but they have very different approaches. Dickson states: "it can hardly be said that communications regarding an economic transaction of sex for money lie at, or even near, the core of the guarantee of freedom of expression. " He is probably right in the traditional sense and probably Lederman would agree with him. Nevertheless, if you asked people whether sexual expression or political expression was more important to them, my guess is that a lot of them wouldn't go the Lederman/Dickson route.

Wilson takes a different approach, stating: "economic choices are ... for the citizen to make (provided that they are legally open to him or her) and as such deserve constitutional protection "whether the citizen is negotiating for the purchase of a Van Gogh or a sexual encounter." She takes a different approach, again on a normative basis although a different one than Dickson.[14]

CONCLUSION

Professor Lederman's work set the stage in many ways for the Supreme Court's first approaches to freedom of expression questions under the *Charter*. Both Lederman and the Court share the same traditional liberal norms. Having said that, I think we can still say that Lederman's analytical framework provides a jumping-off point for greater practicality in fundamental freedom decisions, reflecting the Canadian propensity for "accommodating" individual freedom while protecting the social fabric.

I have canvassed some links between the Court and Lederman's analyses: political speech is considered central; there is an abstract view of freedoms and rights; American tests and concepts are relied on heavily. Despite all this, both Lederman and the Court have focused a great deal of their consideration on section 1 of the *Charter*. This focus on the limits of freedom of expression in a free and democratic society rejects American absolutism. Further, the focus on section 1 has included some attempt to consider other *Charter* values when interpreting the limits on freedom of expression.

I suggest going further along these lines. It is possible to develop a more "made in Canada" approach by continuing to focus on what limits apply to freedom of expression in our society, however this focus could now shift beyond section 1. It could now include a linking of the substantive right in section 2(b) to other *Charter* rights, in particular equality rights and the other fundamental freedoms themselves. This would result in a more workable, less abstract conception of freedom of expression at the first stage of defining section 2(b) prior to section 1 testing. I would argue that this would be a natural extension of Lederman's mutual modification doctrine. Lederman's ideas of judicial and legislative lawmakers as partners, not rivals, also provides inspiration for more pro-active use of the *Charter*. I would say that his awareness of contextuality and the practical possibilities of limitation and regulation of freedoms sets the stage for impact-oriented, collective rights-based decisions. We have seen the beginnings of this in the freedom of expression area in the cases of hate literature and obscenity. So, again (for those not still reeling from my suggestion that Bill Lederman might end up being called feminist) I would say that if in the future we begin to see the concerns of marginalized communities more valued in Supreme Court opinions, if we begin to see a more Canadian characterization of fundamental freedoms as bound up with collective interests, if we begin to see judicial decisions that mandate active intervention, we will owe some thanks to Bill Lederman.

NOTES

1. A. de Mestral et al., eds., *The Limitation of Human Rights in Comparative Constitutional Law*, (Cowansville, Quebec: Editions Y. Blais, 1986).
2. [1986] 2 S.C.R. 573.
3. W. R. Lederman, *Continuing Canadian Constitutional Dilemmas* at 406-7.
4. *Ibid.* at 407.
5. *Ibid.*
6. *Ibid.* at 406.
7. *Ibid.* at 410.
8. *Ibid.* at 411.
9. *Edmonton Journal v. Alberta (A.G.)*, [1989] 2 S.R.C. 1326 at 1355.
10. D. Lepofsky, *The Supreme Court's Approach to Freedom - Irwin Toy v. Quebec (Attorney General) - And the Illusion of Liberalism* (1993) 3 N.J.C.L. 37.
11. Lederman, *The Concurrent Operation of Federal and Provincial Laws in Canada* (1963) 9 McGill L.J. 185.
12. *Supra*, note 10.
13. (1993) 2 Dal. J. Leg. Stud. 251.
14. David Dyzenhaus did a piece for the *Ottawa Law Review* in 1991 suggesting that in both of these decisions the judges are really expressing their values with respect to prostitution, where they see prostitution rather than real constitutional values which they might in fact agree on: D. Dyzenhaus, "Regulating Free Speech" (1991), 23:2 Ottawa L. Rev. 289.

Freedom of Expression: Hate Propaganda, Pornography, and Section 1 of the *Charter*

Kathleen Mahoney

I would like to thank the Queen's University Law Faculty for inviting me to attend this symposium in honour of the late Professor Lederman. I did not have the good fortune to work with ProfessorLederman, but I certainly am aware of many of his major accomplishments and contributions to the law, and I am very honoured to take part in this event today.

When I was invited to attend I was asked to discuss issues of freedom of expression, hate propaganda and pornography in the context of section 1 of the *Canadian Charter of Rights and Freedoms*.[1] Since Professor Lederman was such a proponent of the view that Canada must develop a uniquely Canadian constitutional jurisprudence, I thought it would be interesting to look at these issues by contrasting and comparing them to American law.

Section 1 of the *Charter* is the central, pre-eminent provision. Its function is to define our society and its direction. It gives meaning to constitutional guarantees by requiring judges to examine them in the context of the social and political life of Canada. When rights collide, as they do in the race and sex vilification context, judges must decide what abstract concepts, such as freedom of expression and equality, really mean and then determine the appropriate balance between them.

Section 1 states that the *Charter* "guarantees the rights and freedoms set out in it subject only to such reasonable limits prescribed by law as can be demonstrably justified in a free and democratic society." This is an unusual section if one compares it with other national or international rights-protecting instruments. The American *Bill of Rights*, for example, has no similar section. At first glance, section 1 may appear to be inconsistent or contradictory. On the one hand it guarantees rights, yet on the other hand it authorizes limits on those rights. The presence of section 1 in the *Charter* requires the analysis to be split into two distinct stages. The first stage requires a court to determine the scope and content of the right, and then to decide whether the right has been breached. In the second stage, the court determines whether any limitation on the right can be justified in the context of the free and democratic society of Canada. This double function embodies the idea that constitutional rights in the *Charter* are not absolute. This has been borne out in a number of freedom of expression cases, but most notably in the race and sex vilification cases.

When the Supreme Court decided to uphold legislation limiting freedom of expression in order to protect women and racial minorities from discrimination, many Americans gasped in disbelief.[2] Politically, I think Americans see our conservatism as liberal, our liberalism as socialist and our socialism as beyond the pale. But constitutionally, when our Supreme Court decided to interpret our guarantees of freedom of expression contrary to First Amendment values, many Americans seem to have thought that we had lost our grip completely. I experienced this personally because I was interviewed by telephone by numerous interviews and supposedly objective members of the American press. These individuals found it very difficult to disguisetheir incredulousness at the perceived assault that these decisions represented to Western culture, especially the perceived assault on the civil libertarian culture of rugged individualism, on the social and economic culture of unbridled capitalism, and the assault on the sexist and racist culture of subordination and violence. But regardless of the particular focus of their questions otherwise, they were unanimous in asking the question, "Why did the Canadian Supreme Court do this?" Some of the more thoughtful even asked, "How did they do it?"

I think a partial explanation is the general view taken by our Supreme Court that freedom must have a social as well as an individual meaning, and that power and freedom are inextricably linked.

One of our greatest judges and intellectual leaders of the Supreme Court, Madame Justice Bertha Wilson, has spoken of this. Looking at the role of government in Canadian society when comparing Canadian to American attitudes she said,

> Canadians recognize that government has traditionally had and continues to have an important role to play in the preservation of a just Canadian Society. ...It is, in my view, untenable to suggest that freedom is co-extensive with the absence of government. Experience shows the contrary, that freedom has often required the intervention and protection of government against private action.[3]

The tradition of parliamentary supremacy, and the basic desire for a just society, does not adequately explain the truly radical doctrinal metamorphosis that these judgments on freedom of speech represent.

The recognition by the Court that hate propaganda and pornography harm equality rights was a metamorphosis. Favouring equality in the balance against freedom of expression was truly radical. In my opinion it moved our country into a different time zone of jurisprudential concepts. Essentially, the cases stand for the broad proposition that an individualistic approach to rights is not the only, the best, or the most democratic way to resolve all issues when individual rights clash with group or class rights. The Canadian Supreme Court is saying that if the exercise of individual speech rights go so far as to destroy other constitutional group-based rights, particularly equality rights, then the government is entitled to intervene and legislate, regulate, or otherwise mediate between opposing interests. Where pornography is a concern, the speech interests of pornographer are balanced against equality rights of women and children. Where hate propaganda is concerned the balance is between the speech interests of white supremacists and the equality interests of targeted minorities. In other words, the Court recognizes that these are not cases where the government is the sole protagonist infringing upon an individual's rights. Rather, the Court sees the government as mediator between competing interests, making a reasonable assessment as to where a line should be drawn. The relative burdens of the parties would seem to require pornographers or white supremacists to justify limiting equality rights, just as the Crown should have to justify limits on freedom of expression the laws create.

Another explanation to these radical decisions is the entrenchment, in 1982, of the *Charter of Rights and Freedoms*. In my view this was a watershed event in the evolving culture of Canada. With the advent of the *Charter*, Canada became a different kind of society. Not only did our legal culture change, our social culture changed too. We are no longer a democraticfederation whose constitutional antagonists are just federal and provincial governments, fighting over powers. In 1982, the people of Canada got a piece of the constitutional action. Equality seekers in particular, after the most massive grassroots lobbying effort ever experienced in Canadian legal history, achieved an amazingly comprehensive set of equality rights, guaranteeing them equality before and under the law, and equal protection and equal benefit of the law.[4]

In addition, an affirmative action provision was entrenched,[5] as well as a blanket guarantee of gender equality in the exercise of *Charter* rights.[6] Further, a multiculturalism clause mandates that the *Charter* be interpreted in a manner consistent with the preservation and enhancement of the multicultural heritage of Canadians.[7] While the latter does not confer substantive rights, the crucial interpretation process in section 1 is significantly influenced by the provision.

Thrust upon the courts to interpret and implement, this new regime brought about a significant reordering of the political balance of power in the country. It also provided a clean, unencumbered, constitutional slate for the courts not only to reflect upon and correct past embarrassing mistakes made under the *Bill of Rights*,[8] but develop the law in a principled manner, consistent with our own 21st century self-image of pluralism and democracy.

The desire to forge a new and uniquely Canadian constitutional jurisprudence is clear in judicial comments from the early days of *Charter* interpretation. Former Chief Justice Dickson and others urged at the outset that care be taken to avoid mechanical application of concepts developed in different cultural and constitutional contexts, in different ages, and in very differentcircumstances.[9] American jurisprudence, in particular, was targeted for comment.[10]

Justice Wilson, for example, quite pointedly criticized the American school of thought which promotes the "framers' intent" interpretation of constitutional law. She said the following:

> Why should a group of men, and I stress men, long since deceased be allowed to constrain the progressive development of the American constitution? Why should they put it into an 18th century straight jacket?

> ...My point here, can be underlined by a simple thought experiment. Let us ask ourselves what the United States framers intent was on the issue of the rights of women. We must keep in mind that we are talking about a period long before women had the right to vote, a period when married women had no legal existence separate and apart from their husbands. ...Surely women's rights were not high on the agenda of the framers of the American constitution.Well haven't times changed? Today's approach to women's rights is informed by an overall societal commitment to sexual equality ... And yet, if we took the framers' intent school seriously, we would be forced to [admit that today's societal commitment does not reflect] an original constitutional truth. Thus we can see that in certain circumstances it would be unthinkable to allow the framers' intent to govern constitutional interpretation.[11]

So instead of developing the "framers' intent" approach, the Canadian Supreme Court firmly adopted a purposive approach to constitutional interpretation.[12] Justice Wilson describes this approach as based on the premise that the purpose of the *Charter* is to protect those typically shut out of the political process, namely the poor, the oppressed, the powerless, and racial minorities.[13] She said judges must ask themselves how a climate can be created in which the quality of life of all Canadians can be enhanced and their aspirations for self-fulfilment fully realized.[14] Her veryclear and consistent message is that the true test of rights is how well they serve the less privileged, and the least popular, segments of society.[15]

Another strong theme developed early in *Charter* jurisprudence was the principle that the interpretive, balancing exercise in section 1 must be dynamic rather than static.[16] The "living tree" metaphor adopted for constitutional interpretation was tied to the community's normative framework with the view that if community norms nourish constitutional principles, the constitution will evolve in a way sensitive to societal change.[17] This approach is meant to avoid the creation of rigid doctrinal principles that may not serve us well in the future. To the extent that the American approach to constitutional law relies on the intent of the framers and fixed doctrinal concepts such as those underlying the First Amendment, the dynamic Canadian approach is quite different.

Justice Rosie Abella of the Court of Appeal of Ontario describes equality in this vein. She says:

> Equality is evolutionary in process as well as in substance. It is cumulative, it is contextual and it is persistent. Equality is, at the very least freedom from adverse discrimination. But what constitutes adverse discrimination changes with time, with information, with experience, and with insight. What we tolerated as a society one hundred, fifty or even ten years ago is no longer necessarily tolerable. Equality is thus a process, a process of constant and flexible examination, of vigilant introspection and aggressive open mindedness.[18]

Translated into doctrine, this approach requires that any constitutional analysis be results oriented. In one of its earliest *Charter* decisions, the Court said that a law would violate the *Charter* if either its purpose or effects were contrary to the freedoms guaranteed by the *Charter*.[19] This requirement forced the courts to be concerned with the historical, cultural, economic and social facts of the cases and how they inter-related with constitutional issues. The analysis grew even deeper as *Charter* history unfolded.

The most profound effects of the purposive approach are seen in the cases which directly or indirectly engage equality rights. In their first opportunity to define discrimination and equality and to address the scope of the equality guarantee, the Supreme Court saw the role of the *Charter* not as neutral on inequality, but rather as having a commitment to end it. The monumental decision to jettison the similarly situated test of discrimination, saying that it was so unprincipled it could justify Hitler's Nuremberg laws, was the clearest indication that a paradigm shift wasunder way.[20] Sweeping away centuries of accepted law, the Court opened the door to real, substantive change. The new test measures discrimination in terms of social, political and economic disadvantage rather than sameness and difference. Procedurally, it provides an escape from abstract, formal rules and doctrinal straight jackets created by the similarly situated test. Effectively, it situates constitutional law right in the middle of the messy reality of life. Women and disadvantaged minorities can tell courts why they are persistently disadvantaged whether that be because of sexual violence, pornography, pregnancy, racism, homophobia, unequal pay, lack of reproductive self determination or any other systemic barrier. Shining constitutional light on these facts makes the failings of the system so obvious that it forces prejudice concerning women and disadvantaged groups out into the open and sometimes out of the law.

The context-based analysis is the key to understanding the decisions in race and sex-based hate propaganda cases. Once the courts adopted the purposive approach and decided it required a contextual analysis, the door opened for women and minority groups to make their case for constitutionally supportable regulation of racial hate speech and pornography in section 1.

Let me turn to the cases themselves. In 1990, three cases were appealed to the Supreme Court challenging the constitutionality of hate propaganda laws.[21] *Regina v. Keegstra*[22] was heard in conjunction with two similar appeals, *Regina v. Andrews and Smith*[23] and *Canada (Human Rights Commission) v. Taylor*.[24] *Keegstra* and *Andrews* raised the same issue: the constitutional validity of section 319(2) of the *Criminal Code*,[25] a provision that prohibits the wilful promotion of hatred, other than in private conversation, towards any section of the public distinguished by colour, race, religion, or ethnic origin.[26] *Taylor* raised the issue of theconstitutional validity of section 13(1) of the *Canadian Human Rights Act*, a legislative provision that prohibits the communication of hate messages over the telephone.[27]

In all three cases the Court was asked to decide whether the legislation infringed the guarantee of freedom of expression found in section 2(b) of the *Charter*, and, if so, whether it could be justified under section 1 of the *Charter*. Of the three, *Keegstra* was the leading decision in that it set out the approach adopted by the majority in the other two cases. I therefore will confine my remarks to the reasoning of the Court in that decision.

In *Keegstra*, the accused, James Keegstra, a high school teacher, used his classroom time to communicate anti-semitic teachings to his students.[28] He was convicted at trial of the offenceof the public, wilful promotion of group hatred.[29] The conviction was appealed to the Alberta Court of Appeal, where it was unanimously overturned, the Court finding that section 319(2) of the *Criminal Code* unjustifiably infringed Keegstra's freedom of expression as guaranteed by section 2(b) of the *Charter*.[30] Speaking for the court, Judge Kearns found that, although deliberate lies are not protected by section 2(b), innocently or negligently made hate speech is. Moving to the section 1 analysis, he said that, while he accepted that section 319(2) had the valid legislative objective of preventing harm to the reputation and psychological well-being of target group members, he nevertheless found the section unconstitutional because the injury was not serious enough to require the sanction of criminal law. In order to be constitutional, more than reputational harm was required. Greater harm, such as proof of actual hatred being caused as a result of the impugned expression, was necessary. Sections 15 and 27 of the *Charter*, the equality and multicultural sections, were not viewed as justifying the hate propaganda laws under section 1. This decision was appealed to the Supreme Court of Canada.

To determine whether or not the hate propaganda prohibition violated the *Charter*, Chief Justice Dickson, writing for the majority, first examined the scope to the freedom of expression section. He did so by looking at the underlying values supporting the freedom of expression guarantee. Those values, he said, are seeking and attaining the truth, encouraging and fostering participation in social and political decision-making, and cultivating diversity in forms of individual self-fulfilment and human flourishing.[31]

After finding the scope of section 2(b) to be both large and liberal, the Court adopted a strict categorical test,[32] permitting content-based restrictions only if the speech is communicated in a physically violent form.[33] Otherwise, as long as an expressive activity conveys a meaning, it isprotected by section 2(b), regardless of the meaning of message conveyed. The Court held that even threats of violence are within the scope of the section's protection.[34] Governments may restrict expressive activity only when their purpose is other than to restrict the content of the activity. Even if the purpose is directed solely at the effect rather than the content of the expression, section 2(b) can still be brought into play if the affected party can demonstrate that the activity in question supports, rather than undermines, the principles and values upon which freedom of expression is based.[35]

Applying this categorical test to the hate propaganda provision, Chief Justice Dickson found that the legislation prohibiting the public, wilful promotion of group hatred did indeed infringe section 2(b) of the *Charter*. He said the hate propaganda provision was an attempt by Parliament to prohibit communication conveying meaning. The Chief Justice made the point that competing values contained in other *Charter* provisions, such as equality, multiculturalism, and Canada's international obligations to prohibit hate propaganda, should not be balanced within the freedom of expression guarantee at the first stage of analysis. This was because the Court would not have the benefit of making a contextual assessment and the analysis would be dangerously and overly abstract.[36] He said that it was preferable to assess the balance of competing values under section 1 because that would permit a contextual analysis that fully weighed the harm hate speech inflicted on minorities.

Having determined that the public, wilful promotion of group hatred as a category fell within the protection of section 2(b) and that the criminal prohibition infringed James Keegstra's freedom of expression, the Court turned to consider whether under section 1 the infringement was a reasonable limit demonstrably justifiable in a free and democratic society. The Court split four to three in finding that the burden of section 1 was satisfied and that the legislation could be upheld.

The analysis followed in the format set out by *Regina v. Oakes*.[37] In determining that the impugned law relates to pressing and substantial concerns, three reasons were articulated. The first focused on the harm caused by hate propaganda, the second on the importance of equality and multiculturalism, and the third on Canada's international obligations. In dealing with the first, Chief Justice Dickson stressed that extremist hate speech is not merely offensive; it causes "real" and "grave" harm to both its target groups and society at large. Like sexual harassment, hate propaganda constitutes a serious attack on psychological and emotional health. Members of the target groups are humiliated and degraded, their self worth is undermined, and they are encouraged to withdraw from the community and deny their own personal identity. The majority described hate propaganda's societal harm as causing serious discord between cultural groups and creating an atmosphere conducive to discrimination and violence.[38] The passage provided one of the clearest indications that the Canadian Court was moving away from American constitutional law. Its rejection of the clear and present danger test as a method of determining the constitutional validity of the legislation allowed a different assessment of harm. The Court said that the American test should not be used because it was incapable of comprehending the subtle and incremental ways that hate propaganda works. "Shouting fire in a crowded theatre", the Court is saying, has nothing or very little to do with the type of harm the law and the *Charter* seek to address. The Court recognized that the clear and present danger test would render any hate propaganda law almost useless. It predetermines the result because direct, linear immediate harm through speech seldom occurs. Even if it does, it is impossible to prove because of the cognition required before action takes place.

Instead, a broader definition of harm was adopted. It includes harm to listeners, to members of the target group and to the fundamental democratic value of equality. Of these harms, the finding that hate propaganda harmed the democratic value of equality was clearly the most legally significant because it allowed the Court to consider the constitutional relevance of equality-promoting legislation.

In a potentially far-reaching statement, the majority said the application of the equality guarantee is not confined to actions by individuals against state — imposed discrimination. It is also relevant in assessing the validity of legislation which promotes equality rights but may at the same time infringe other constitutional rights. This meant that the *Charter* can be used as a shield to protect legislation, as well as a sword to strike it down. It also meant that equality rights are relevant in determining the scope and content of the freedom of expression guarantee in the section 1 balancing. Here, the government action to prohibit hate propaganda received special constitutional consideration because it promoted social equality.

While the Court admitted that the muzzling of the hate promoters undeniably detracts from the freedom of expression value, the degree of harm to those values is minimal compared with the degree of harm to other values[39]. The majority situated multicultural values in an equality context, saying that attacks on groups need to be prevented because group discrimination can adversely affect its individual members.[40] According to the Court, in restricting hate propaganda, Parliament seeks "to bolster the notion of mutual respect necessary in a nation which venerates the equality of all persons."[41] This reasoning is not dissimilar to that of the United StatesSupreme Court in *Beauharnais v. Illinois*,[42] to which the Chief Justice referred, suggesting that the *Beauharnais* decision is closer to the Canadian approach to freedom of expression than the line of cases that subsequently undermined it.[43] The Chief Justice cautioned that even though current American free speech doctrine may be helpful in many respects, it is of dubious applicability in the context of a challenge to hate propaganda legislation.

The Chief Justice is entirely correct on this point. The *Charter* is not constrained by the textual or political constitutional imperatives of the American first amendment. More importantly, the fundamental structural, historical, and circumstantial differences between the two constitutions require a distinctively Canadian approach.[44] Although both countries share a democratic ideal, they do not share the same view of social and political life. In sociological terms, Canada and the United States experience some of the same realities of heterogeneity of population, of language differences, and of an original native population.[45] In this dimension, definition and reconciliation of minority rights have been central to civil liberties politics in both countries. A major ideological difference is Canada's rejection of the melting pot approach to cultural diversity adopted in the United States in favour of a mosaic approach. One of the objectives of the drafters of the *Charter* was to develop a bilingual, multicultural country and a pluralistic mosaic.[46]

As a result, *Charter* commitments are different in many respects from the commitments of the American Bill of Rights. The multicultural section is a case in point. Section 27 states that the *Charter* shall be interpreted in a manner consistent with the preservation and enhancement of the multicultural heritage of Canadians.[47] This provision is particularly important when courts are required to balance the freedom of expression of hate propagandists against the multiculturalism ideal and the powerful equality provision. It is thus much broader in scope than the Fourteenth Amendment, containing wider substantive protections as well as more prohibited grounds ofdiscrimination. Reading section 15 together with the multiculturalism section creates a formidable obstacle for those who would use the freedom of expression guarantee to promote hatred against identifiable groups.

The other minority interests protected in the *Charter*, including language and education rights, aboriginal rights, and rights for denominationally separate dissentient schools[48], underline the strong commitment to collective rights in the *Charter* that is not evident in the American Constitution. Against this background, it is not surprising the Court found that prohibition of the public, wilful promotion of group hatred is a matter of pressing and substantial concern sufficient to meet the section 1 requirements.

To emphasize furhter the point that hate propaganda laws relate to pressing and substantial concerns, the Court took note of international human rights obligations that require Canada to suppress hate propaganda criminally to protect identifiable and vulnerable groups.[49] The Court said that when values such as equality and freedom from racism enjoy status as international human rights, they are generally ascribed a high degree of importance under section 1.[50] The United States has not ratified this or similar conventions. With respect to the proportionality requirement of section 1, the Court balanced the freedom of expression guarantee against the content of the hatemonger's speech. By examining the values underlying the freedom of expression guarantee: the search for the truth, participation in the political process, individual self-development and human flourishing, and then carefully considering the circumstances surrounding both the use of the freedom and the legislative limit, the majority found that the hate propagandists' expression was of limited importance. They said it not only fails to promote freedom of expression values, it works against them. Neither the quest for the truth nor self-development and human flourishing are enhanced. The fostering of a vibrant democracy is subverted because of the attack on participation in the political process. Any political aspect of hate propaganda loses its democratic aspirations when it argues for the subversion of the democratic process.[51]

The rational connection test was also met because the Court found that although hate propaganda laws cannot prevent a Holocaust, their worth as part of a free and democratic society's bid to prevent the spread of racism has been demonstrated by anti-hate laws in other jurisdictions. It was also thought important that to members of target groups, the criminal prosecution of hatemongers reassures them that racist ideas are rejected and their equality is affirmed.

On the minimal impairment criteria, the majority concluded that the law is not overbroad because while it prohibits the public, wilful promotion of group hatred, it exempts statementsmade "in private conversation", whether in public or in private.[52] The subjective *mens rea* requirement protects conversations which may become public through accident or negligence.

The mental element of "wilfulness" further narrows the law in that it applies only where an accused subjectively desires the promotion of hatred, or foresees that hatred is certain or substantially certain to result from the statements made. On the meaning of the word "hatred", the Court said it must be defined according to the context in which it is found. It must go beyond distastefulness to reach the extreme form of dislike, vilification, detestation and malevolence that belies reason. These elements of the offence combined with the defences of truth, expressions of good faith and honest belief on religious subjects, and public interest, make the provisions sufficiently explicit and clear to address concerns about the "rough and tumble" of public debate.[53]

As to alternative modes of furthering the objectives of Parliament, the majority was of the view that a variety of measures must be employed to foster tolerant attitudes. Government may legitimately employ more, as well as less, restrictive measures as long as they are not redundant.

In conclusion, the majority found that the law satisfied each of the components of the section 1 test. The entire Court found the purpose of the law to be of great importance. A majority of four found it to be proportional to its objectives. It is neither overbroad, nor too vague. As well, it is eminently reasonable for the state to utilize more than one legislative tool to prevent the spread of racist expression and its resultant harm.

In summary, the approach established by the *Keegstra* decision in the section 1 balancing stage legitimated group rights to the extent that they outweighed the competing individual right of freedom of expression. This was due to the influence of section 15.[54] The recognition that the harm of discrimination can outweigh the free speech interest marks a major new development in freedom of expression jurisprudence. The connections the Court made between institutional arrangements, collective and individual harms, human relations, and equality are unique. The Court's recognition that boundaries between individual and collective rights must be confronted demonstrates the *Charter's* potential to propose new relationships.

Canada's departure from American free speech doctrine is clear. Under the first amendment, social reality is not considered when legislation regulating extremist speech is challenged.[55] This is a critical difference from the Canadian practice because, depending on the facts of the case, a contextual analysis can result in a right or freedom having a different value. In *Keegstra*, when assessing the value of challenged expression, the Court looked at the reality of the situation at hand, including the nature of the interests at stake. The centrality of equality to theenjoyment of individual as well as group rights in the decision demonstrates a firm acceptance of the view that equality is a positive right, that the *Charter's* equality provision has a large remedial component, and that legislatures should take positive measures to improve the status of disadvantaged groups. Most importantly, *Keegstra* identifies a transformation potential in the *Charter*. This is a potential to achieve social change toward the creation of a society based on an ethic that responds to needs, honours difference, and rejects abstractions.

Turning now to the issue of pornography, the leading case of *R. v. Butler*[56] arose in 1987 when Mr. Butler and an employee were charged with some 250 violations of the obscenity provisions of the *Criminal Code*. The accused challenged the definition of obscenity as a violation of his freedom of expression guaranteed by the *Charter*. The definition reads as follows:

> any publication, a dominant characteristic of which is the undue exploitation of sex, or of sex and any one or more of ... crime, horror, cruelty and violence, shall be deemed to be obscene.

By the time the case reached the Supreme Court of Canada, the *Keegstra* case had been decided. Even though it was a close 4-3 decision, the idea that expression could be more than speech, that it could amount to discrimination, was the crucial breakthrough which established a legal foundation to argue in *Butler*, that pornography could be constitutionally regulated on a harms-based equality analysis.

The same method of analysis as that used in *Keegstra* applied to determine the constitutionality of obscenity laws. First, the scope of freedom of expression was examined to see if the legislation violated the expression guarantee. Finding that it did, it was then tested against the section 1 standard to see whether it constituted a reasonable limit prescribed by law, as can be demonstrably justified in a free and democratic society. On the basis of *Keegstra*, an equality, harms-based theory was able to regulate pornography constitutionally under sections 1, 2(b), 15, and 28 of the *Charter*.

The contextualized approach to equality adopted by the Supreme Court in *Andrews* established that the sex equality interest in pornography's regulation arises out of the harms it causes.

As section one's function is to balance tensions between harms, the state was required to prove that the rights or interests protected by the law outweigh the expression right infringed. The equality approach adopted in *Keegstra* required a balancing of the harms that flow from regulating expression by obscenity laws against harms actualized through the promotion of women's inequality in pornography. In deciding on the proper balance, the Court was guided by the values and principles essential to a free and democratic society, which include respect for the inherent dignity of the human person, commitment to social justice and equality, accommodation of a wide variety of beliefs, respect for cultural and group identity, and faith in social and political institutions that enhance the participation of individuals and groups in society.[57]

The section 1 analysis required several steps. First, the objectives of the obscenity provisions had to be shown to be of sufficient importance to warrant overriding the constitutionally protected right of freedom of expression in pornography.

Second, once the objective was established, the state was required to show that the means chosen to attain the objective could be reasonably and demonstrably justified in a free and democratic society. To conclude that the means chosen are reasonable and demonstrably justified, the Court had to be satisfied of three things: The measures designed to meet the legislative objective were rationally connected to the objective; the means used impaired as little as possible the right and freedom in question; and there was proportionality between the effect of the measures that limit the *Charter* right or freedom and the legislative objective.[58]

Here, pornography made a stronger case for regulation than hate propaganda did. Pornography is much more commonplace, socially accepted, and widely distributed across class, race, and geographical boundaries than hate propaganda is, and it exists in a societal context of pervasive sex inequality. It follows that the harm of pornography must be deeper, wider, and more damaging to social life than the harm of hate propaganda.[59]

Although he Court did not redress individual harm, pornography often involves real violence where women are coerced and sexually assaulted so that they become the subjects of pornography.[60] When overt infliction of pain, overt use of force, or the threat of either of them is used in the production of pornography, its purely violent nature should take it outside of any *Charter* protection such that no section 1 balance should be necessary. To fail to do so would improperly dignify and to some extent legitimize a vicious trade. Furthermore, mass marketing of sexual assault as a form of entertainment provides a profit motive for physically harming people. Clearly this is a more serious, immediate harm than the harms identified by the majority in *Keegstra*. Pornography that is made from assaults should be no more worthy of protection as expression than the assaults themselves.

In dealing with broader, societal harm, the discriminatory effects of pornography were obvious. When the Court inquired into the larger social, political and legal context of women's experience it was easy to see how the rape, battery, prostitution, incest and sexual harassment that thousands of women endure contribute to their unequal status with men.

The encouragement and promotion of subordination in pornography in this broader context, particularly the depictions of violence and exploitation of women at the hands of men, reinforces the systemic violence and the social harm.

Stereotyping and stigmatization of historically disadvantaged groups were recognized as harms deserving of sanction in *Keegstra* because of the Court found that they shape the social image and reputation of group members, often controlling their opportunities more powerfully than individual abilities do. The vast proliferation and sheer volume of pornography compared to hate propaganda makes the harm to women's credibility, safety, and opportunities much more serious and generalized.[61]

The pressing and substantial concern requirement was further bolstered by section 28. As noted above, section 28 states that, "notwithstanding anything in the *Charter*, the rights and freedoms referred to in it are guaranteed equally to male and female persons." Once the Court made the initial finding that pornography could not be excluded from section 2(b) protection, the guarantee of sex equality within section 28 fell to be contemplated within section 1. It is unfortunate that the Court chose not to explain the interaction between s.28 and s.1, although it would seem to be straight forward. According to section 28, sex equality is unconditional. As such, it cannot be tempered by any other provisions in the *Charter*. What this means is that section 28 must weigh in the balance of section 1 to the extent that no freedom or right should override legislation when it would have the effect of increasing sex inequality. Once the discriminatory effects of pornography are understood, it follows that freedom of expression cannot be expanded within section 1 where the effect will be to perpetuate or promote women's subordinate status.[62] Furthermore, treating the state goal of eliminating sex discrimination as forming a reasonable justification for limiting free speech[63] should allow a cutting back of fundamental freedoms in section 1 in order to reinforce equality or combat sex inequality. An explanation, by the Court of the effects of s.28, its purpose and effect in the *Charter* is long overdue. *Butler* provided a perfect opportunity but for some unknown reason the Court chose not to grasp the moment. As it is such a potentially powerful factor in the operation of section 1, it is indeed unfortunate that Canadian women still await a careful and reasonable interpretation of "their section".

After finding that the obscenity legislation met a pressing and substantial objective, the test of proportionality was applied. Here, the Court considered not only the importance of freedom of expression and the significance of the limitation, but also whether the way the limitation was imposed was justifiable. Obscenity laws were found to have a rational connection to women's equality because of the harm pornography causes. By prohibiting violent, degrading anddehumanizing forms of pornography, Parliament was promoting women's equality. Similarly, the laws met the minimal impairment test. The Court examined the definition, the defences and the burden of proof of the obscenity law and concluded that the net was not cast too wide. In shifting the emphasis from sexual morality to safety and protection of women's rights, the law was much more constitutionally defendable. Parliament's reasonable assessment as to where to draw the line is given more deference when the purpose of the legislation is to protect reasonable groups from harm.

For example, Justice Sopinka, writing for the Court, said that the harms analysis makes it untenable to argue that time, place, and manner restrictions are a better form of regulation that prohibition. This reasoning is correct because imposing heavy taxes on pornography, or requiring special licences for its distribution sends the message that harms to women will be tolerated as long as the user pays. Government would be complicit in the pornography trade and even become a participant in it if it collected taxes or issued licences. Justice Sopinka pointed out how inconsistent and hypocritical it is to argue time, place, and manner restrictions once the state has reasonably concluded that certain acts are harmful to certain groups in society. To permit such acts as long as conditions are more restrictive is wrong because the harm sought to be avoided remains the same in either case.[64] This approach is encouraging because it means that the *Charter* is not neutral on practices that promote inequality. Rather, it is a constitutional commitment to ending them.

The suggestion that reactive solutions such as the provision of counselling for rape victims are more proportional to the objective than prohibition also lose their force once harms are recognized. As alternatives to prohibition, they imply that women must absorb the harm caused by the very behaviour encouraged by pornography. It is hard to believe that such a requirement could have any credibility in any society that is free and democratic and has equality as an entrenched guarantee. Certainly these and other strategies should be offered to protect women from violent men, but to argue, as the civil liberties intervenors in the *Butler* case did, that they are preferable to controlling the dissemination of the very images that contribute to such behaviours diminishes the harm and consequently diminishes women and children as full citizens. As the Court stressed, serious social problems such as violence against women and children requires a multi-faceted approach.[65]

The final portion of the *Oakes* test required the Court to examine the proportionality between the effect of the obscenity laws on freedom of expression and the legislative objective. The Court examined the relationship of pornography to the free expression values of seeking and attaining the truth, participation in social and political decision-making, individual self-fulfilment and human flourishing.

Not surprisingly, it was found that, like hate propaganda, pornography is low-value speech. The Court was not persuaded that opinions advocating the sexual violence or degradation of women in pornography will lead to a better world or can contribute to truth-seeking. The Court was mindful of the messages in pornography that say women and children are sex objects available to be violated, coerced, and subordinated at the will of men and replicated in real life statistics that appear to be increasing at a rapid rate. In the Court's view, the "value" of pornography as a truth-seeking device was minimal or perhaps, non-existent.

It seems reasonable to conclude from the Court's decision that when forms of speech seek to subvert the truth-seeking process itself, the interests of seeking truth work against rather than in favour of it.[66]

The harms of pornography render it antithetical to the other values and purposes underlying the freedom of expression guarantee as well. In terms of the value of self-fulfilment, for example, if individuals who traffic in and consume pornography are fulfilled, it is at the expense of the rights of women. Human flourishing of men cannot be said to be encouraged by material that harms women.

Libertarians argued in the case that the harm of pornography is in the eye of the beholder and any offensiveness caused is easily diminished or eradicated by averting the eyes or not listening. The problem with this argument was that it misunderstood the Court's understanding of the true essence of discrimination, which is not how members of disadvantaged groups feel about themselves, but rather how they are viewed by members of the dominant majority.

To the extent that the majority of *Keegstra* made a clear finding that degradation and humiliation fall into the category of serious harms rather than mere offensiveness, the pornographers were unable to argue that pornography's harms are trivial or within the victims' control. In *Keegstra*, the harms caused by hate propaganda were analogized to the harms of sexual harassment, an individualized harm that also promotes group disadvantage.[67] Pornography's harms, which affect women as a class as well as individual women, should have been analogized to sexual harassment as well. The parallels are stronger and the harms are at the very least, equivalent.

Another aspect of pornography and its links to hate propaganda which the Court unfortunately did not discuss in the section one examination was the combinations of terms of vilification in the same portrayal. For example, rape portrayals where race religion, age and sexual orientation are a factor. The sexualization of racism, homophobia, sexism or the vulnerability of children must increase the quotient of harm in a synergistic way. Multiple discrimination has been acknowledged for its greater harms in many other contexts. There is no reason for it to be ignored in the pornography context. As the abuse of minority women is common in pornography where their other vulnerabilities are exploited in addition to their sex, this is an issue which must be addressed.

In summary, the Courts recognition that the sexual exploitation of women and children can lead to "abject and servile victimization" as well as other types of harm goes some way toward redistributing speech rights between men and women. The Court's contextually sensitive method of defining pornography and its harms in the *Butler* decision is a welcome development in the law that other countries and the international human rights community should contemplate if they are genuinely serious about women's human rights, violence against women and women's equality. As virtually all pornography in Canada comes from the United States, it would be particularly helpful for Canadian women if the American Supreme Court were to re-think some ofthe stagnant, grand principles of the First

Amendment which never included consideration of women in their making and as a result, fail to deliver complete justice.

NOTES

1. *Constitution Act, 1982*, Part 1.
2. See *Regina v. Keegstra*, [1990] 3 SCR 687; *Regina v. Andrews and Smith*, [1990] 3 SCR 870; *Canadian (Human Rights Commission) v. Taylor*, [1990] 3 SCR 892; *R. v. Butler*, [1992] 1 SCR 432.
3. *McKinney v. Board of Governors of the University of Guelph* (1990), 76 DCR (4th) 55 (SCC) at pp. 582-83. See also *Reference Re Public Service Employee Relations Act (Alta)*, [1989] 1 SCR 313 at 67 *per* Dickson, CJC.
4. Section 15(1) reads as follows: "Every individual is equal before and under the law and has the right to the equal protection and equal benefit of the law without discrimination and, in particular, without discrimination based on race, national or ethnic origin, colour, religion, sex, age or physical or mental disability."
5. The affirmative action clause, s.15(2) reads: "Subsection (1) does not preclude any law, program or activity that has as its object the amelioration of conditions of disadvantage individuals or groups including those that are disadvantaged because of race, national or ethnic origin, colour, religion, sex, age or mental or physical disability."
6. Section 28 states that "notwithstanding anything in this *Charter*, the rights and freedoms referred to in it are guaranteed equally to male and female persons."
7. Section 27 provides that the *Charter*, "shall be interpreted in a manner consistent with the preservation and enhancement of the multicultural heritage of Canadians."
8. For example, see *Attorney General of Canada v. Lavell*, [1974] SCR 349; *Bliss v. Attorney General of Canada*, [1979] 1 S.C.R. 1990 where a narrow interpretation of equality resulted in the perpetration of inequality for native women and pregnant women.
9. See *R. v. Rahey*, [1987] 1 SCR 588 at 639; *R. v. Keegstra*, [1991] 2 WWR 1 at 37 (Dickson CJC) and Bertha Wilson, "The Making of a Constitution: Approaches to Judicial Interpretation," Edinburgh, 1988.
10. *Ibid.*
11. *Ibid, per* Wilson, J.
12. *Hunter v. Southam Inc.*, [1984] 2 SCR 145 at pp 155-6 (Dickson CJC) and *R. v. Big M Drug Mart Ltd.*, [1989] 1 SCR 295 at 344 (Dickson, CJC).
13. Actual results of *Charter* litigation have been beneficial for disempowered, often neglected, groups in Canadian society. See *Re Singh and Minister of Employment and Immigration* (1985), 17 D.L.R. (4th) 422 (S.C.C.) which benefitted refugees; *Edwards Books and Art Ltd. et al. v. R.* (1986), 35 D.L.R. (4th) 1 (S.C.C.) which benefitted non-unionized workers; and *Morgentaler, Smoling and Scott v. R.* (1988), 44 D.L.R. (4th) 385 (S.C.C.) which benefitted women. Many others could be cited.
14. Bertha Wilson, "The Making of a Constitution", Address to the Ninth Annual Conference of Women Judges, Seattle, Washington, (October, 1987) at p.12 (unpublished).
15. *Ibid.*
16. Brian Dickson, *The Horace E. Read Memorial Lecture, 1991*, "Madam Justice Wilson: Trailblazer for Justice" (1992), Dalhousie L.J. 1 at 17.
17. *Ibid.*

18. Rosalie Abella, "The Evolutionary Nature of Equality" in K.E. Mahoney and S.L. Martin, eds., *Equality and Judicial Neutrality* (Toronto: Carswell, 1987) p.4.

19. *R. v. Big M Drug Mart* (1985), 18 D.L.R. (4th) 321 (S.C.C.).

20. *Andrews v. Law Society of British Columbia*, [1989] 1 S.C.R. 143.

21. *Supra*, note 2

22. [1990] 3 SCR 697.

23. [1990] 3 SCR 870.

24. [1990] 3 SCR 892.

25. *Criminal Code*, R.S.C. 1985, c. C-46, s. 319(2).

26. *Ibid.*, The relevant provisions of section 319 read as follows:

    (2) Every one who, by communicating statements, other than in private conversation, wilfully promotes hatred against any identifiable group is guilty of

       (a) an indictable offence and is liable to imprisonment for a term not exceeding two years; or

       (b) an offence punishable on summary conviction.

    (3) No person shall be convicted of an offence under subsection (2)

       (a) if he establishes that the statements communicated were true;

       (b) if, in good faith, he expressed or attempted to establish by argument an opinion upon a religious subject;

       (c) if the statements were relevant to any subject of public interest, the discussion of which was for the public benefit, and if on reasonable grounds he believed them to be true; or

       (d) if, in good faith, he intended to point out, for the purpose of removal matters producing or tending to produce feelings of hatred towards an identifiable group in Canada.

       ...

    (6) No proceeding for an offence under subsection (2) shall be instituted without the consent of the Attorney General.

    (7) In this section,

       "communicating" includes communicating by telephone, broadcasting or other audible or visible means;

       "identifiable group" has the same meaning as in section 318 [("any section of the public distinguished by colour, race, religion or ethnic origin," id § 318(4))];

       "public place" includes any place to which the public have access as of right or by invitation, express or implied;

       "statements" includes words spoken or written or recorded electronically or electromagnetically or otherwise, and gestures, signs or other visible representations.

27. *Canadian Human Rights Act*, RSC, 1985, c. H-6, s. 13(1), as amended.

28. The accused taught social studies courses to students in grades 9 and 12 at Eckville High School from the early 1970s until 1982. Through evidence given by former students, as well as students' notebooks and essays written during courses, it was determined that the accused taught anti-semitic theories. Students were expected to take down what was said by the accused in class or written by him on the blackboard, and they were expected to learn and reflect thisinformation in the form of essays and on exams. If their essays and exams contained the theories taught by him in class, they received excellent marks. If, however, they used sources from outside his classroom such as encyclopedias, dictionaries, and history books, they received poor grades.

The accused taught only his personal biased views and told the students they should accept his biased views as truth unless they could contradict them. Statement of Facts, Appellant's Brief, Her Majesty the Queen at 2, *Keegstra*, [1990] 3 SCR 697.

29. *R. v. Keegstra* (1984), 19 C.C.C. (3d) 254 (Alta QB).

30. *R. v. Keegstra* (1988), 87 AR 177 (CA).

31. *R. v. Keegstra*, [1990] 3 SCR at 727, relying on *Irwin Toy Ltd v. Quebec (Attorney General)*, [1989] 1 SCR 927, 976, aff'g *Ford v. Quebec (Attorney General)*, [1988] 2 SCR 712, 765-67).

32. *Id.* at 728-29.

33. In *RWDSU v. Dolphin Delivery Ltd*, [1986] 2 SCR 573, 588, the Supreme Court ruled that the freedom of expression guarantee does not extend to acts of violence and threats of violence. In *Keegstra*, the Chief Justice, writing for the majority, clarified this exception, ruling that only meanings communicated throughthe medium of violence will be excluded from s. 2(b) protection. *R. v. Keegstra*, [1990] 3 SCR at 731. The minority opinion, authored by Justice McLachlin, maintained that threats of violence fall outside s. 2(b) protection. *Id.* at 826-27.

34. Reference re ss. 193 and 1985. 1(1)(c of the *Criminal Code of Canada*, [1990] 15 CR 1123, 1181; *Keegstra*, [1990] 3 SCR at 732. Justice McLachlin, joined by Justices LaForest and Sopinka in dissent, however, held that threats of violence do not attract § 2(b) protection. *Ibid.* at 830-31.

35. *Keegstra*, [1990] 3 SCR at 762.

36. *Id.* at 764-70.

37. [1986] 1 SCR 103,136.

38. *Keegstra*, [1990] 3 SCR at 744-49.

39. The Court cited Cory J. (as he then was) in *R. v. Andrews* (1988), 65 OR (2d) 161, where he said, "if free rein is given to the promotion of hatred, multiculturalism cannot be preserved let alone, enhanced."

40. *Keegstra, supra*, note 2 at 746.

41. *Id.* at 756.

42. 343 U.S. 250 (1952).

43. *Anti-defamation League of B'nai B'rith v. FCC*, 403 F2d 169, 174 (DC Cir 1968); *Colin v. Smith*, 587 F2d 1197, 1204-05 (7th Cir 1978).

44. *Re BC Motor Vehicle Act*, [1985] 2 SCR 486, 498; compare to *Collin v. Smith*, 587 F2d 1197 (7th Cir 1978).

45. For a further discussion, see Alan F. Westin, "The United States Bill of Rights and the Canadian Charter: A Socio-Political Analysis", in William McKeacher, ed, *The U.S. Bill of Rights and the Canadian Charter of Rights* 27 (Economic Council, 1983).

46. *Special Joint Committee of the Senate and House of Commons on the Constitution of Canada: Final Report* (Ottawa: Queen's Printer, 1972). The minutes state that the purpose of a multicultural provision would be "[t]o develop Canada as a bilingual and multicultural country in which all its citizens, male and female, young and old, native peoples and Métis, and all groups from ethnic origins feel equally at home."

47. *Charter*, section 27.

48. *Charter*, sections 21, 25, 35, 29.

49. See article 4 of the *International Convention on the Elimination of All Forms of Racial Discrimination* (New York, Aug. 24, 1966), entered into force for Canada, Jan. 4, 1969, *Canada Treaty Series*, 1970, No.28.

50. *Keegstra*, [1990] 3 SCR at 750, citing *Slaight Communications Inc. v. Davidson*, [1989] 1 SCR 1028, 1056.

51. *Keegstra*, [1991] 2 W.W.W. 1 at 56 (SCC).

52. *Ibid.*, at 62.

53. *Ibid.*, at 71.

54. Justice Wilson in *R. v. Turpin*, [1989] 1 SCR 1296, 1333, said that § 15 is designed to protect those groups that suffer social, political, and disadvantage in our society.

55. See *Doe v. University of Michigan*, 721 F Supp 852 (ED Mich 1989); Penelope Seator, "Judicial Indifference to Pornography's Harm: *American Booksellers v. Hudnut*", (1987), 17 Golden Gate U L Rev. 297.

56. [1992] I SCR 432.

57. *Oakes*, [1986] 1 SCR 103.

58. *Keegstra*, 3 SCR at 735-38 (Chief Justice Dickson). In his discussion of the role of Section 1, the Chief Justice also stressed that it is misleading to conceive of Section 1 as a rigid and technical provision. He said it plays an immeasurably richer role embracing not only Charter values, but all values associated with a free and democratic society. There must be an awareness of the synergistic relationship between the values underlying the Charter and the circumstances of the particular case.

59. See *Metropolitan Toronto Task Force on Public Violence against Women and Children, Final Report* 74 (1984) ("*Metro Final Report*"); Diane E.H. Russell, "Pornography and Rape: A Causal Model", 9 Political Psych 41 (1988); "Pornography and Violence: What Does the New Research Say?", in Lederer, ed, *Take Back the Night* at 218; Malamuth & Donnerstein, eds, *Pornography and Sexual Aggression*; Donald L. Mosher & Harvey Katz, "Pornographic Films, Male Verbal Aggression Against Women, and Guilt", in 8 *Technical Report of the Commission on Obscenity and Pornography* (US Govt Printing Office, 1971); Macmanus, "Introduction", *Report of the Joint Select Committee on Video Material, Commonwealth of Australia* (Aust Govt Publishing Service, 1988).

60. *Final Report of the Attorney General's Commission on Pornography* 747-56, 767-1035 (U.S. Govt Printing Office, 1986) ("*Final Report*").

61. Thelma McCormick, "Making Sense of Research on Pornography", in *Metro Final Report, supra*, note 59, at 37.

62. Lahey, Kathleen A., "The Canadian Charter of Rights and Poronography: Toward a Theory of Actual Gender Equality" (1984-85), 20 New Eng L Rev 649 at 683.

63. *Ibid.*, at 683..

64. *R. v. Butler*, *supra*, note 2, at 62.

65. *Ibid.*, at 61.

66. See Lee Bollinger, *The Tolerant Society: Freedom of Speech and Extremist Speech in America* (Oxford U Press, 1986) pp. 87-93 .

67. In *Janzen*, [1989] 1 SCR 1252, Justice Dickson drew a clear connection between sexual harassment and sex inequality generally.

PART FIVE

CRIMINAL LAW

Post-*Charter* Omne Animal Triste?

Christine Boyle

I was delighted to be asked to speak at this symposium in honour of Professor Lederman, whom I remember with great respect from my time here at Queen's as a graduate student in the early seventies. I'm very pleased to have been given the opportunity to add my voice to those of others who have spoken of him with such warmth.

I want to say a few things about the impact of the *Charter* on criminal law, drawing on the rhyme about the little girl who had a little curl right in the middle of her forehead. When she was good she was very good and when she was bad she was horrid. Well what I want to suggest is that when the *Charter* is good it is not very good, and when it is bad it is certainly horrid. Rooted as it is in established notions of criminal law and procedure, it's transformative power is limited. It's as if not just heterosexual sex but the missionary position suddenly got constitutionalized.

I'll touch on a couple of examples, which I hope will show the limited potential for criminal law to be developed through progressive *Charter* challenges. The first one comes from the work I have been doing on corporate liability for homicide. It's quite clear that the construction of the "appropriate accused" in a homicide prosecution is much more likely to involve an individual than a corporation, more likely to be Donald Marshall than Curragh Inc. in the Westray mine disaster. This is a huge issue but I'd like to make two points about it.

First, there are issues of fair enforcement practices here which I would say are largely out of reach of a *Charter* challenge. If I wanted to tilt the enforcement of criminal law away from relatively disadvantaged human beings to corporations who profit from killing or even to the state itself, I don't see how I could do that. I don't see how I could protect the disadvantaged, given fears of anarchy, and I don't see how I could force the prosecution of the privileged, given the fact that *Charter* challenges seem to be the prerogative of the defence. I notice Don Stuart made this point but I had already planned to quote *Charter Justice in Canadian Criminal Law* in support of this point.

> Thus far courts have resisted attempts to use the s.15 equality guarantee as a protection against discriminatory law enforcement in a particular case....The lack of success of such claims thus far suggests criminal courts will continue to be inadequate forums for consideration of such serious, but difficult to substantiate, charges as racism.[1]

It's certainly not a new point that those decision-makers who are most important to accused persons and probably victims too, the police and sentencing judges, are most immune from *Charter* accountability with respect to fundamental questions of the overall fairness of the criminal justice system. Legislative decisions seem more vulnerable to scrutiny, for instance in the context of the debate over subjective and objective tests. Yet even here the scrutiny does not go very deep. If one of the major achievements of the *Charter* is that Parliament is not allowed to call people "murderers" who take guns with them while committing robberies, where someone gets shot, then I think it is fair to say that we have not embarked on any fundamental rethinking of the values reflected in the criminal law.

Second, there is the substantive law with respect to use of the criminal law of homicide in the context of business killings of workers and consumers. One of the barriers to proving homicide under the criminal law is the need to prove a causative link between the act or omission and the death. As Celia Wells points out, in *Corporations and Criminal Responsibility*, there are obvious practical problems in holding businesses responsible for the damage inflicted on employees or the wider public by toxic material used in production processes or products.[2] The limits of scientific and medical knowledge certainly create problems in proving causation. The *Charter* can't do anything about that, but there are substantive, as well as practical, reasons why causal indeterminacy is an immense barrier to criminal responsibility in this context. If the substantive law is structured in such a way as to include unprovable elements in many cases, then the criminal law will exhibit systemic under-reporting of homicidal activity. So the present law, with its focus on the actual causing of death rather than on death-risking activities, (which I might add was what constructive murder was aimed at) plays a role in focusing attention on individual deaths, rather than on multiple deaths associated with economic activity.

It seems to me that it is a political, rather than a constitutional approach, which is more likely to produce a rethinking of basic doctrine linked to systemic bias in the criminal law. However, having said that, I haven't seen much interest in such rethinking with respect to recodification of the general principles of criminal law. For instance, should a corporation be liable for causing death by criminal negligence through failure to carry out its duties under provincial law, the issue raised in the Westray prosecution? The answer to this question will form a part of the overall picture which will readjust the focus of the criminal law in terms of both individual liability and workers' safety. However, the Report of the Sub-Committee on the Recodification of the General Part of the Criminal Code (of the Standing Committee on Justice and the Solicitor General) did not address this issue.

So that is one point — the *Charter* is unlikely to be good enough to force examination of the deeply-rooted assumptions underlying our notions of who is an appropriate criminal. When its good it's not very good. When is it horrid? For an example, I turn to the concept of a fair trial for the accused, when used as a weapon against women. My impression is that there is some tendency (perhaps wishful thinking by defence lawyers) to assert that Canada has a profound commitment to the right to a fair trial, and that this commitment has been strengthened by constitutionalization. I would suggest that we have a rather tentative commitment, except where social forces other than the *Charter* are at work, and that change will not be dramatic. For instance, an accused has a right to retain counsel, but no guarantee of effective or competent counsel, or that will engage in the supposedly adversarial process, or even of one who is qualified under legal aid schemes. An accused has a right to trial by jury for serious offences but an aboriginal person, as Don Stuart points out, has no right to be tried by aboriginal peers. There is a system at work here which allows vast numbers of charges to be processed affecting accused who don't even understand, unrepresented or represented by someone who will not fight for their interests or who will only do so if they are white and paying. I don't see the *Charter* at work changing the depressing picture painted by Canadian criminologists. Nevertheless, fair trial rights become very significant when attempts are made to improve the law of sexual assault.

While the *Charter* purports to guarantee women's equality and security of the person, in my view it is difficult to argue that the *Charter* has been a positive force in this area. I see it more as a constant source of threat to improvements in the law, rather than as a means of enhancing women's status and safety.

I'd like to use the on-going story about a sex-equal concept of relevance in sexual assault prosecutions as an example, and draw on a case I have been working on recently, *R.v.O'Connor*.[3] The story is one of continuing political efforts to improve the treatment of sexual assault complainants opposed by some judges, an opposition now strengthened by the *Charter*.

I'll start the story with Wigmore, a U.S. evidence theorist still very influential in the Canadian legal system. In his book *The Principles of Judicial Proof as Given by Logic, Psychology, and General Experience*,[4] he included material supporting the idea that sex, race and age are relevant to credibility. For instance, "[d]ishonesty is, however, a specially feminine quality; in men it occurs only when they are effeminate."[5]

Our ideas of relevance have changed but not because of any improved theories, rather because there has been a shift in what we could call common sense. Aside from writers such as Wigmore, judges have developed the legal notion of relevance as setting the outside boundary on what is admissible in trials, including sexual assault trials. They are no more sophisticated than Wigmore, and determinations of relevance are largely a matter of hunch and guesswork, thus creating a breeding ground for prejudicial assumptions about particular groups in society. The admissibility of evidence of the victim's sexual history in sexual assault trials is a good example. Parliament entered the story by trying to limit the use of such evidence, but again there was no apparent theory, just exclusionary rules.

So as you know, the Supreme Court of Canada in *Seaboyer*,[6] using the right to a fair trial, struck down these limits. We still had no theory of relevance. All the participants in the developing this law had thus far proceeded simply by assertion. The Supreme Court of Canada asserted that sexual history was sometimes relevant, and again simply asserted that instances of such relevance would be rare and that sexual history was not by itself relevant to consent or credibility.

Seaboyer is not just horrid in that the *Charter* was used to hand control back to the judiciary, who are supposed to know better than Parliament. This was achieved even though both politicians and judges were simply arguing by assertion, and the outcome depended just on whose assertion was more legally authoritative, that is, who can shout the loudest. *Seaboyer* is also a good illustration of the *Charter's* deficiencies. For example, the *Charter* can't make us any smarter than we already are. If discriminatory assumptions about certain groups (in the case of sexual assault, women and children) are imbedded in our notions of relevance, and we are incapable of eradicating such notions intellectually, and then must rely on who can shout the loudest to resolve disputes, a heightened legal significance attached to certain shouts may only do harm. Wigmore promoted such ideas as Eskimos are prone to lie and Jews are less credible than Christians. I hope that such ideas no longer have any influence on our law, but to the extent these ideas disappeared they went without the help of the *Charter*.

Further, a U.S. style Bill of Rights with its emphasis on the need to address disparities of power between the individual and the state, may not be capable of addressing more complex interacting inequalities, both among individuals and among communities. The majority in *Seaboyer* addressed the issue of validity of the exclusionary evidentiary rule as if it were only a question of fairness, as opposed to an issue requiring an analysis of the co-existing rights to a fair trial and the right to the equal protection and benefit of the law. Indeed, I cannot find a case in which the Supreme Court has given any guidance on how to construct co-existing rights. Even in *Butler*,[7] equality only appears as a s.1 limit on freedom of expression. Freedom of expression and freedom from discrimination both have to be given meaning within the one constitutional document. The unidimensional understanding of the imbalance of power between the accused and the state, while a very important one, has to intersect with an understanding of other imbalances of power. So far the *Charter* hasn't increased our ability to grasp more than one imbalance of power at a time. Again, the extent to which intersecting inequalities have been theorized has been more a political than a constitutional process.

To continue the story of the admissibility of evidence of the victim's sexual history, Parliament came back into the picture with Bill C-49, which, roughly speaking, codifies *Seaboyer*, so complainants are still dependent on judicial, non-theorized, non-complex notions of the relevance of sexual history. No doubt the *Charter* will be used to challenge Bill C-49, if indeed that has not happened already.

Currently, in litigation the ground has shifted to the pre-trial stage and the effects of *Stinchcombe*[8] on pre-trial disclosure in sexual assault trials. The accused is entitled to disclosure of relevant information. The issue in *O'Connor*[9] is whether therapists' records are relevant. I fully expect the outcome to be horrid in that women and children will be expected to make an extraordinarily onerous contribution to what is assumed to be, untheorized and in isolation from equality, fairness. The best we can hope for is a conclusion that the Crown does not have to hand over information not in its possession, which might be more consistent with the tenuous commitment to fairness I mentioned earlier than with movement toward a sex-equal concept of relevance, which I would have thought should be mandated by the *Charter*, although is not, or is not yet.

My conclusion is not unlike Don Stuart's, in that I am ambivalent. The *Charter* is a great aspirational document which is satisfying on some level. Promises such as liberty and equality not only sound wonderful to people hungry for both, but give disadvantaged groups, and others, the authoritative legal vocabulary to make more assertive legal claims in some contexts. The *Charter* won't of its own motion transform us into fairer or smarter beings, or make society more egalitarian, but it may provide a framework for getting us where we are already prepared to go. Of course, the impact of the *Charter* is just one question in the bigger issue of the transformative potential of law.

In his article in the *Queens Law Journal*[10], Professor Lederman, using the metaphor of judges as referees, took a generally optimistic view of the *Charter*, but added that both referees and players must now pay better attention to the general purposes and objects of the game. I agree.

NOTES

1. Don Stuart, *Charter Justice in Canadian Criminal Law*, Scarborough: Carswell, 1991.
2. Celia Wells, *Corporations and Criminal Responsibility*, New York: Oxford University Press, 1993.
3. *R. v. O'Connor* (1993), 105 D.L.R. (4th) 110.
4. John Henry Wigmore, *The Principles of Judicial Proof as Given By Logic, Psychology and General Experience,and Illustrated in Judicial Trials*, Boston: Little Brown & Company, 1913.
5. *Ibid.*, at p. 335.
6. *R. v. Seaboyer*, [1991] 2 S.C.R. 577.
7. *R. v. Butler*, [1992] 2 W.W.R. 577.
8. *R. v. Stinchcombe*, [1991] 3 S.C.R. 326.
9. *R. v. O'Connor*, (1993), 105 D.L.R. (4th)110.
10. William Lederman,"Democratic Parliaments, Independent Courts and the Canadian Charter of Rights and Freedoms", (1985), 11 Queen's L. J. 1

The *Charter*: "Good" or "Bad" for Criminal Law?

Don Stuart

It's a great privilege to be speaking at an occasion to honour the memory of Bill Lederman. This afternoon Christine Boyle and I intend to explore our differences of opinion on the impact of the *Charter* on criminal law. I am very familiar with Christine's writings and I believe that we hold similar views in a lot of areas, but I'm quite sure that you will see significant differences emerge. Bill Lederman loved a debate, and I'm sure that Christine and I will do him proud this afternoon.

First, a word about Bill Lederman's attitude to entrenching civil rights. He was a sceptic and did not believe in the entrenchment of civil rights. This was evident back to the *Bill of Rights* debates in the 1960's. However, it's very much a testament to the type of man Bill Lederman was, that once we did get an entrenched *Charter of Rights* in 1982, he came to believe that the *Charter* should be made to work. I can remember fondly searching discussions that Bill Lederman conducted with me about the latest *Charter* judgments from courts, including those of his friends Brian Dickson and Bertha Wilson.

From the enactment of the *Charter* I have been what's informally referred to as a *Charter* enthusiast. The *Charter* has certainly revolutionized my life as a law teacher and writer. As Bill Lederman would say, if nothing else the *Charter* has been good for the professor business.

I will first attempt an overall assessment of whether the *Charter* has had a good or bad impact on the criminal justice system, and I will conclude that it's had a positive net impact. Six years ago, I would have said, "the *Charter* has been absolutely marvellous", but now I say, "the *Charter* is much better than nothing". So you can see that my enthusiasm has waned! However, I see three major advantages of having an entrenched *Charter of Rights and Freedoms*.

The first and best argument for having an entrenched *Charter* in the criminal law area may be summed up in the words "Preston Manning". Many in society seem to be increasingly attracted to the lure of law and order politics. It seems much easier simply to toughen the laws against something, rather, for example, than to deploy more resources to crime prevention. Entrenching individual rights protects against law and order, parliamentary expediency. The *Charter* provides some brake on the enthusiasm with which parliamentarians adopt quick fixes.

I have a list of such achievements in applying the *Charter* in the context of criminal law. These achievements have made the criminal law a little softer in these areas. I think I can easily justify each of them.

One of the most important achievements was the setting of a constitutional standard against absolute criminal responsibility. Chief Justice Dickson had got it quite right in a pre-*Charter* decision, *Sault Ste Marie*,[1] when he said the state really has to justify punishing someone when that person has taken all reasonable care. Given the law and order predilections of some parliamentarians, without the *Charter*, in the last few years we would have had a lot of absolute liability offences. For example, in the area of sexual assault, Bill-C49 would have abolished any form of mistaken belief in consent as a defence rather than the much more sensible compromise adopted of recognising a crime based on negligence.

Thus, entrenching the fault principle in criminal law is a very important achievement in applying the *Charter*. A further example has been the abolition of constructive murder. In the years that I've been in Canada that I haven't heard any politician say, "I think it's time to soften the law on murder as the murder laws are too inflexible, and we need a little more leeway so that some accused could be convicted of manslaughter instead of murder". It took the *Charter* and the Supreme Court of Canada to strike down the offence of constructive murder.

Since the 1960's and 1970's a huge debate had raged about the *Criminal Code* abortion provisions. Politicians didn't dare touch them. It took the Supreme Court of Canada applying the *Charter* to strike the provisions down.

When I arrived in Canada in 1970, one of the first things I read was an editorial in the *Globe and Mail* to the effect that the Minister of Justice, Mr. John Turner, had got it right: writs of assistance had to be abolished. Two months later the Government invoked the *War Measures Act* and we put that reform on hold for more than 10 years until writs of assistance were struck down under the *Charter*.

The seven year minimum sentence required for importing marijuana or any other narcotic imposed that sentence for the importation of even one joint of marijuana. Most people said this harsh penalty could not be justified in such cases. However, the minimum penalty remained until it was struck down by the Supreme Court of Canada.

The declaration of a constitutional right to discovery of the Crown's case is very important to accused in criminal cases. Most studies have also established that the criminal justice system is much better off if the Crown fully discloses the case to the other side, one result being that there are many more guilty pleas. When the Supreme Court of Canada recognized the discovery right in the *Stinchcombe*[2] case, it was against the background that Law Reform Commissions had recommended something along those lines but nobody had actually done it. Even the Supreme of Canada didn't recognize an absolute right to discovery. The right was subject to the rules of relevance and privilege.

In another example, criminal law theorists and practitioners had talked about an accused's pre-trial right to remain silent, but it took the Supreme Court of Canada to actually formally recognize it as part of our Constitution.

Another systemic problem of the criminal justice system was delay. People often recoil in horror to the aftermath of *Askov*[3] in which over 50,000 cases were stayed in Ontario. However, if you had been a prosecutor in Ontario's Peel jurisdiction, for example, it wasn't good for anybody when you were setting down trial dates two years in the future. The victims, the witnesses, the accused, and everybody else were forced to wait two years. Every year the Chief Justice of Ontario recognized that delay in criminal trial processes was a problem, but nothing effective was done. Since *Askov* was decided the problem of delay in the Peel jurisdiction is measurably improved. I think that is a significant advance under the *Charter*.

There are other examples of achievements in applying the *Charter*, such as the right to be advised of the right to counsel, and so on.

Now I have a couple of examples of such potential benefits of the *Charter* which may be more controversial, but where I believe minimum constitutional standards are useful safeguards. As I have said, when Parliament may have been too expedient in enacting legislation, I think itsvery good that we have a chance for *Charter* standards to be applied to that legislation at a later stage by the courts. My first example of such hasty legislation stems from the quick enactment of statutory changes in response to the *Seaboyer*[4] decision, striking down the rape shield provisions. This was a largely partisan process of reform in the sense that the voices of women, I think for the first time in Canadian history, were really heard. I also want to say that the politicised process did not offer an opportunity for everybody to fully participate and have their views heard. When I testified to the Parliamentary committee on a couple of occasions I had M.P's coming up to me afterwards saying, "I absolutely agree with you, Professor Stuart, [all I wanted was the creation of two separate offences of deliberate and negligent sexual assault], but I can't say anything". A less contentious example of legislation enacted with haste is the Mulroney Government in its dying days rushing through a whole slew of electronic surveillance provisions with precious little debate.

I would now like to turn to the second of the three advantages of the *Charter*, namely, that it entrenches the view that in the criminal law the rights of the individual accused, in particular the legal rights in sections 7 to 14, must take precedence over other rights, particularly the equality interest of victims. I know this is highly contentious and that it highlights the central difference between my position and what I take to be Christine Boyle's position.

Most women who have read and responded to *Seaboyer* believe that one of the biggest aggravations was that Madam Justice McLachlin said, in a very offhand way, that she recognized that there are equality rights and equality issues but, in the criminal context they are less important than the right to make full answer in defence. I think Madam Justice McLachlin was right. Christine's response to me is going to be, in effect, "Why do you always overlook equality rights, guaranteed under section 15, and overlook that everybody, including victims of crime, have the right to security of the person under section 7?". Christine says you shouldn't talk about balancing rights: they are equal. To me, in the context of the criminal trial, the accused's and the victim's rights are inconsistent at some points and they can't be equal.

I'm not saying that the victim's rights shouldn't be taken into account in reaching interpretations of the scope of the accused's rights. For example, it's my view that the response to the accused's right to discovery issue is indeed to accept that there is a discretionary privilege for certain communications. For example, communications between a victim and her counsellor ought normally be considered privileged.

In a criminal trial the purpose is to decide whether the accused is justly to be punished and perhaps justly sent to jail. In my view important traditional values such as the presumption of innocence, proof beyond reasonable doubt, and the right to make full answer and defence, must take precedence. I have a similar response to the movements to recognize the rights of the victims of crime more generally. Victims have far too long been treated very badly in the criminal justice system and as we get more sensitive, more victim services arise. More governments should impose surcharges on fines and give the proceeds to victim assistance programs. However, in the actual process of deciding whether this accused goes to jail and for how long, the views of the victim could never be determinative. Consider two identical offenders but in one case the victim is forgiving and in the other case the victim is seeking vengeance. Surely, the penalty could not always directly respond to the perspective of the victim? Victims' interests are of importance and are to be considered, but are of lesser importance and are not to be determinative.

The third advantage of the entrenched *Charter* in the criminal justice system is that it makes relevant to a criminal trial, policy issues that were never considered before. I think particularly of policies of holding police officers and prosecutors to some extent accountable. Now I don't want to overstate this. I don't know, for example, of a single case where there has been a successful *Charter* argument that either a police officer or a prosecutor was racially biased. Most will recognize that racism is a huge problem in the criminal justice system in particular, as it is in life in general. It seems that the *Charter* doesn't respond to this problem.

However, the *Charter* has certainly permitted responses to lots of other realities. In the 1960s the eminent jurist, Mr. G. Arthur Martin, said he was opposed to the introduction in Canada of the exclusionary rule for unlawfully obtained evidence. That rule was something developed for the Americans, and it was claimed that it hadn't worked very well down there. The rule was said to be counter productive as many people had complained that it deflected attention from the real issue of the guilt or innocence of the accused. Further, Canada had a very effective alternative, it was said, civil actions against police officers. About 5 years later an American researcher came to Toronto to find out about this great civil remedy against police officers for misconduct. He sought information on how many actions there were and how often these actions were successful. There had in fact only been about 3 cases in 10 years, and only a trivial amount in damages recovered. Compare that to the experience since 1982 in interpreting just one *Charter* right, that under section 8 against unreasonable search and seizure. There are several hundred cases a year dealing with section 8 challenges. If there were no real possibility of excluding evidence obtained contrary to the *Charter*, with some guilty accused being acquitted as a result, nobody would take such rights seriously. In fact, there have been substantial improvements in things like search warrant procedures, and the education of Justices of the Peace, etc.

The *Charter* clearly has a hugely innovative role for the responsibilities of lawyers and judges. Law schools have to be much more imaginative in training students. Gone are the days when the only thing we had to do was to try to find the *ratio* in a case. Yesterday we had a visit to the Law Faculty of Madam Justice Louise Arbour and she pointed out that almost everybody on the Court in Ontario has never been trained about purposive interpretation of legislation and how to examine which interests are protected. Present judges may well be quite resistant to a new way of thinking which wasn't part of their tradition. The *Charter* gives a new avenue into the court room to raise important policy issues. These issues now dominate the criminal justice system and criminal procedure in particular.

What is the downside which leads me to conclude that in the end the *Charter's* impact is only better than nothing? The major problem is that the Supreme Court of Canada is thoroughly inconsistent in applying the *Charter*. I don't think there's any doubt about that and it's not just changing personnel, although the losses of Madam Justice Wilson and Chief Justice Dickson were huge blows to *Charter* enthusiasts. There remain absolutely fundamental questions of principle under the *Charter* that are still quite up in the air. The biggest such question is the proportionality test under section 1. We have this formalistic approach to section 1. We all spout off the *Oakes*[5] blueprint as if it means something. The only key question is, does the limit restrict as little as possible? Courts can't seem to make up their minds whether they are going to stick with the strict *Oakes* test of, as little as possible, used in *Seaboyer*, or whether it is, as little as reasonablypossible, as used in *Edwards Books*[6]. For a while the Supreme Court used the *Chaulk*[7] test: is the lesser restriction as effective? That was over the very strong dissent of Madam Justice Wilson. I think it's the finest judgment in the criminal law that she wrote, and I've always wondered whether she resigned from the Court because she saw which way the right wing winds were blowing. She couldn't convince anybody to take her seriously on the key question of the test for section 1. Fortunately, it would appear that the Supreme Court is backing off the *Chaulk* test and is back to, "does it restrict as little as reasonably possible?". This doctrinal analysis is crucial because the whole balancing of policy interests takes place when the law is on trial under section 1. Given that minimum intrusion is the key test, it is absolutely amazing how fast and loose the Supreme Court of Canada seems to play with it.

The other downside of the *Charter* stems from the increasingly conservative stance of the Supreme Court in the context of criminal law. By that I mean a pro-conviction stance. If the Supreme Court sets the *Charter* standard too low, Parliament won't pick up the slack. I have two examples. This last couple of weeks we've had an absolutely crucial decision in the law of manslaughter. In *Creighton*[8] a bare 5 to 4 majority of the Supreme Court preserved the present law about unlawful act manslaughter, a form of constructive liability which cuts across basic principles of criminal law. The U.K. Law Reform Commission is trying very hard to abolish unlawful act manslaughter and unlawful act manslaughter is not in favour in other jurisdictions. However, if I were to ask the Department of Justice seek a legislative amendment to reverse this decision because it is too severe, I would not have a hope of persuading Justice. I would be dismissed as a soft liberal, a law professor from Disney World, especially as the Supreme Court of Canada said the law was okay. The other example is from same decision, *Creighton*. For a long time there has been a debate about whether the objective standard for fault is, first, appropriate for criminal law, and second, whether it's constitutional. Most academics, including myself, have always said there is room for the objective standard of fault, but in a measured way. The *Creighton* majority opinion includes an offensive interpretation of the objective standard which says that the trier of fact cannot take into account individual factors affecting the accused such as youth, lack of education, and inexperience. That position is flatly contradictory to the much heralded decision of the Supreme Court of Canada in *Lavallee*[9] to take the fact of an abusive relationship into account when applying an objective test for self-defence.

Included in my list of negatives would be that the Supreme Court of Canada has now retrenched on the right to be tried in a reasonable time. Rather than staying 55,000 cases in Ontario we're not staying any now. The test was changed in the *Morin*[10] case. The Supreme Court is extraordinarily conservative on stays of prosecutions as a remedy for an abuses of process. I predict there will be an inevitable build up of delay again, delays which are not in the long term interest of justice, victims, or witnesses. In other negatives the Court has saved every reverse onus clause since *Oakes*, and provided absolutely no protection for double punishment. Also, the *Charter* has been interpreted to have very little impact in the context of prisons, where the concern is for better standards for the treatment of prisoners.

In balancing the positives and negatives the *Charter* does not appear to be anything like a panacea. In the criminal justice system the main reason for saying that the *Charter* has been a good idea is that an entrenched *Charter* affords some balance against law and order expediency. As well, the rights of the accused are recognized as being of paramount importance given the particular brutal reality of the criminal law which occurs when somebody is taken in handcuffs to a prison cell. Finally, the *Charter* focus away from guilt and innocence has allowed for long overdue consideration of such policy issues as police brutality and lack of respect for process.

NOTES

1. *R. v. Sault Ste. Marie (City)*,[1978] 2 S.C.R. 1299.
2. *R. v. Stinchcombe*, [1991] 3 S.C.R. 326
3. *R. v. Askov*, [1990] 2 S.C.R. 1199.
4. *R. v. Seaboyer*, [1991] 2 S.C.R. 577.
5. *R. v. Oakes*, [1986] 1 S.C.R. 103.
6. *R. V. Edwards Books & Art Ltd.*, [1986] 2 S.C.R. 713
7. *R. v. Chaulk*, [1989] 1 S.C.R. 369.
8. *R. v. Creighton*, [1993] 3 S.C.R. 3.
9. *R. v. Lavallee*, [1990] 1 S.C.R. 852.
10. *R. v. Morin*, [1992] 1 S.C.R. 771.

PART SIX

GROUP RIGHTS

Taking Group Rights Seriously

Jacques Frémont

INTRODUCTION

I had the privilege of meeting Bill Lederman at a conference held in Quebec City, about ten years ago. I was immediately struck by the profound humanity of this great Canadian scholar. He was not only one of the leaders of the first generation of constitutional academics in Canada, but was also obviously a friend of Quebec. He was indeed concerned by what was happening at this time in Quebec in the aftermath of the patriation debate. I, like most Quebec constitutional lawyers, still regard Bill Lederman's writings as models of conceptually clear, intelligent and imaginative academic writing.

In getting prepared for this Conference, I had the opportunity of re-reading all Bill Lederman's writings about "group rights". They show a remarkable concern to find compromises in this conceptually difficult area of constitutional law. It has to be remembered that these texts were written in a period during which rights in general and group rights in particular were not in the spotlight, and at a time when group rights were simply ignored. Today things have changed as while group rights may have become generally unpopular, they cannot be ignored anymore. Professor Lederman's writings show a great sensitivity towards the question of the protection of the French language in Quebec, while attaching the utmost importance to freedom of expression as an individual right. He seemed to fear Quebec's independence. This fear might explain his openness towards the renewal of the Canadian constitution.

However, this re-reading of Bill Lederman's writings about group rights also shows how much the constitutional universe has changed in Canada over the last 15 to 20 years. Of course, the rights' culture has been greatly enhanced by the adoption of the *Canadian Charter of Rights and Freedoms* in 1982 (the "*Charter*"), but a more specific group rights culture has clearly emerged since the early 1970's. Linguistic minority groups within and outside Quebec have been very much part of the political and judicial debates. Confessional rights have also been debated extensively and more recently, aboriginal rights have occupied the centre field. These various instances of reassertion of group rights have also led the courts to play a crucial role in the definition and the materialisation of group rights. Recent political and constitutional events, such as the aborted Meech Lake and the Charlottetown rounds of formal constitutional reform, the unresolved and pressing question of aboriginal rights, and the discourse of the Reform party about minority rights, all demonstrate that group rights cannot be taken for granted and more than ever have to be taken seriously.

The aim of this short paper is to assess the state of group rights in 1993 and to share some reflections about the difficulties they raise and their future. Of course, for the sake of this discussion, group rights will be examined essentially in a constitutional context; they must be considered as a well established feature of the Canadian constitutional system, despite what many people want to believe. Conceptually and semantically, "group rights" must be distinguished from "collective rights", the latter referring to the whole collectivity, rather than to a group or to the members of a group to which group rights attach. Group rights often imply a positive duty for the state to intervene in order to enforce and respect such rights. This is the case, for instance, in the *Constitution Act, 1867*, s. 93, as far as the issue of schools is concerned in Quebec and inOntario, in s. 133 concerning some linguistic rights, or, more recently in s. 23 of the *Charter*.

In this paper will I first examine briefly the traditional approach to group rights in Canadian constitutional law. I will then discuss the issue of the relationship between the groups and their individual members, the question of the judicial assessment of group rights and, finally, the necessary assertion of group rights by the groups themselves.

GROUP RIGHTS IN THE CANADIAN CONSTITUTIONAL ORDER

We tend to forget that group rights have pre-dated individual rights in Canada. In fact, they have been part of the constitutional order since 1867 and have been the object of litigation and debates since. Since 1982, the adoption of the *Charter* has forced a re-examination of the understanding of group rights in imposing a forced co-existence of constitutionalised rights of a different nature and purposes. While individual rights are firmly anchored within a liberal vision of the state, group rights must be seen and understood, as the Supreme Court reminded us in *Société des Acadiens*[1], as resulting from compromises. They are attributed to specific groups at specific moments in time, and one of the crucial roles of the courts is often subsequently to interpret and adapt these rights to the evolving societies to which they apply.

Group rights are relatively numerous in the Canadian constitutional order. Historically, they subdivide in two generations, by era of emergence. The first generation is that of the original Canadian constitution, as adopted in 1867. Section 93 of the *Constitution Act, 1867* guarantees confessional rights in the provinces of Ontario and Quebec. The main difficulties concerning such group rights, at least as perceived from a contemporary Quebec perspective, flowed from a gradual divorce of the parameters of the rights as guaranteed, and of the sociological characteristics of a society and of the groups which have come to define themselves over the years more in terms of the languages they speak rather than the religions they practice[2].

The other major group right enshrined by the *Constitution Act, 1867* was of course that in s. 133 which guarantees, in Quebec and at the federal level (and, since 1982, in New-Brunswick), some linguistic rights in the legislative and judicial arenas. The history of the evolution and understanding of these rights is too well known and too long to be told again here. However, the reality is that such group linguistic rights were applied by Quebec and Ottawa, while similar rights were systematically ignored by Manitoba and other provinces to which they also applied, although for different reasons and in different contexts.

The second generation of constitutionalised group rights emerged in 1982. The various group rights so enshrined are still in the initial phase of their interpretation, where over and above the letter of the constitutional provisions, a meaning has to be attributed by the political actors to which they apply, with the final word belonging to the courts. The first such right is that of section 23 of the *Charter* which enshrines minority language education rights within Canada by granting them to individuals ("citizens of Canada"). Despite such an explicit, and naive, individualistic approach to the conception of the right attributed, the wording of this provision was interpreted by the Supreme Court of Canada in *Mahe*[3] as involving a group component:indeed, parents belonging to the minority group also have the right to manage and control their educational facilities. This approach rightly demonstrates that when individuals are members of a group, their individual rights must necessarily, in order to be meaningful, carry a group dimension as well. In other words, group rights cannot be hidden exclusively in an individual rights disguise and, inversely, some individual rights may involve a group rights component.

This attempted distinction between granting rights directly to groups or to individuals was again a matter of some discussion when the Canadian constitution was recently modified in order to grant equality of status and of rights to the linguistic groups in New Brunswick. Section 16.1(1) of the *Constitution Act, 1982* as adopted in 1993, recognises rights in the communities themselves rather than in the members of such groups[4]. The same approach was also adopted in 1982 for the recognition and the affirmation of the existing aboriginal and treaty rights of aboriginal peoples in s. 35 of the *Constitution Act, 1982*).

Other less group-explicit provisions are found in s. 27 of the *Charter* which establishes the "preservation and enhancement of the multicultural heritage of Canadians" as a *Charter* interpretative principle as well as in s. 36 of the *Constitution Act, 1982*. While it is still unclear whether the former section creates rights *per se*, it is fairly clear that the latter section, by its programmatory character, does not create rights, at least in the of traditional justiciable nature[5].

From this extremely brief review of the group rights contained in the Canadian constitution, a few conclusions can be drawn. First, and despite their relative un-popularity in some quarters, group rights have been very much part of the constitutional scene since the early days of Confederation and their emergence has accelerated in recent years. Second, it is also clear that the mere entrenchment of group rights has been no guarantee that the group rights in question would not be violated or ignored. The *Manitoba Language Rights* judicial saga[6] is a testimony to the systematic violation of the letter and of the spirit of the entrenched constitutional rights of groups. A third lesson is that group rights have to be entrenched if they are to have any serious impact. The Alberta and Saskatchewan language rights cases are examples of group rights not constitutionally secured and therefore susceptible of being suppressed, as they weresubsequently in these provinces with the explicit blessing of the Supreme Court of Canada[7]. If group rights are not constitutionally entrenched, they can become victims of changing *rapports de force*, thus denying their very purpose which is to protect the characteristics of vulnerable groups.

FROM GROUPS TO INDIVIDUALS

One of the basic questions associated with the concept of group rights is the identification the beneficiaries of such rights. In other words are these rights aimed at protecting the groups themselves, the members of the groups, or both? If the philosophical issues raised by this question are by no means easy to solve, the legal answers might be somewat simpler. As Bill Lederman's writings demonstrate, the answer to the question lies far from the simplistic and doctrinaire views advocated by many today.

It is of course no accident that the wording of s. 23 of the *Charter* attributes linguistic minority education rights to the persons themselves, rather than to the communities. This was Pierre Trudeau's deliberate attempt to deny the importance or the relevance of groups to the Canadian society. The irony with this approach is that, literally interpreted, it leads to a denial of any institutional support to the groups concerned and to an absence of organised and protected means for these groups to effectively support the full exercise of the formally individual rights of their members. It explains why a more realistic attitude fully justifies the attribution of rights to the groups themselves. This attitude also recognises that in many cases the effective realisation of individuals' rights necessarily has to commute through institutions and structures. In fact, Pierre Trudeau's rigid rights-liberalism led, at least in the case of minority language rights, to diminished rights for their beneficiaries, the substance of the rights being for most purposes defined by the ungenerous decisions of the majority.

It explains why, over and above the individualistic wording of the constitutional provision, group or collective dimensions have been added, thus co-codifying the essence of the constitutional requirement without violating the spirit and the purpose of the provision. This enlargement which for most purposes was done through judicial decisions (in *Mahe* or *Manitoba Public Schools Reference* cases[8], for instance) was thus important in demonstrating that contradiction does not necessarily flow from such situations. In fact, and Bill Lederman's writings are a testimony in that respect, there is no fundamental contradiction between individual and group rights in the vast majority of instances. The rights in presence are only of a different nature. Of course, in the cases where they are nevertheless contradictory, they will call for conciliation, as all norms of the same hierarchical order should. It is thus submitted that individual rights and, therefore, the rights of individuals should not intrinsically be considered as superior to group rights.

The constitutional industry and most politicians often tend to forget that the conciliation process must remain the prime responsibility of the political actors themselves. Recent constitution-making history indicates that group rights are more or less exclusively understood in terms of justiciability and of judicial intervention. The problem with such an attitude is that politicians are relieved of responsibility and inherent cynicism follows. This was evidenced by the suppression of linguistic rights seen in Alberta and Saskatchewan and, of course, by the systematic ignoring of such rights over a long period of time in Manitoba before 1985. A disquieting conception of the rule of law is revealed where the question about rights is asked more in terms of discovering how not to be caught out by the courts, than in terms of honestly arbitrating the rights in question. The issue of what the proper role of the courts must be in this respect should nevertheless be examined briefly.

JUDICIAL ASSESSMENT OF GROUP RIGHTS

In the light of years of judicial interpretation and application of group rights, and in recent times of intensive intervention of the courts, the lessons which can be drawn are positive in the sense that courts have been relatively successful in achieving a proper role with respect to the interpretation and application of group rights. Their official interpretative attitude is that of a liberal and purposive approach in line with the attitude adopted in individual rights. Of course, it must be pointed out that the teleological approach might in some respects be seen as a double-edge weapon in such a context. While the advantages of this approach are in allowing, in some cases, a certain return to the original purpose of the right or to the reasons for its emergence (which is useful, therefore, to sustain a reassessment of the right's objectives), and, in other cases, in providing a judicial method for adjusting rights over the years and centuries. The danger in the approach is the risk that the courts might adopt a restrictive judicial attitude similar to the original intent doctrine developed by the American Supreme Court.

The relatively successful track record of the Canadian courts in interpreting group rights should not lead to the conclusions that judicial enforcement is the solution to all wrongs and that judges should be regarded as the ultimate saviours of group rights. The judicial role in this forum is, to say the least, delicate, as acknowledged by Mr Justice Beetz in *Société des Acadiens*, and as quoted in the *Manitoba Schools Reference*, in 1993: "[...] courts should pause before they decide to act as instruments of change with respect to language rights [...] in my opinion, the courts should approach them with more restraint than they would in construing legal rights." One of the reasons explaining this relative hesitation probably has to do with the main difficulty present, that of the remedies available. How can compliance be forced by the courts in such matters? The logic of the *Forest* and *Blaikie* cases[9] was fundamentally ignored by the Manitoba Legislature, and francophones from Manitoba have had to wait until the *Manitoba Language Rights Reference* decision before their rights were finally, literally forced upon a recalcitrant Manitoba Legislature. Paradoxically, one can point out that this very decision which had the effect of re-establishing the language rights of Franco-Manitobans, also officially sanctioned the violation of their rights during the intermediary period until the translation of all statutes was to be completed. In the recent *Manitoba Public Schools Reference*, one wonders what can happen, indeed what will happen, if the Legislature, ultimately, does not follow theparameters defined by the Supreme Court in its ruling? The basic problem in such cases is for the courts to decide whether to impose a solution or else, to leave a certain margin of manoeuvrability to the political authorities. In the *Manitoba Public Schools Reference* (at p. 860), Chief Justice Lamer chose the latter and stressed that the Court did not want "to detail the legislation which the Government must enact to meet its constitutional obligations". It is a very far cry from the open attitude towards judicial remedial powers adopted by the same court a few years before in the *Schachter* case, as far as the sanction of individual rights was concerned.

It is probably fairly difficult for Canadian courts to force compliance with the type of positive constitutional obligations imposed upon the state with respect to group rights. The obvious solution would be that of enforceable judicial orders, with the difficult dimension of having the courts defining its orders to the very last detail and subsequently checking their enforcement and, if need be, by ensuring that the proper financial means are levied through taxation or otherwise. Legitimacy issues would then be crucial and courts could very well be perceived, whether it is true or not, as going too far down the legislative road.

Part of the irony about judicial intervention concerning group rights in recent history is that it might have been too successful, at least in some respects. From now on, as evidenced by the Charlottetown debates about aboriginal rights and the then proposed deadlock-breaking mechanism, groups are constantly and confidently seeking courts to define or reassert their rights. They must not forget, however, that there are no guarantees that the courts will always adopt such generous and liberal attitudes. Recent lower court rulings in Canada about aboriginal rights and titles should be considered as a reminder of that fact. Indeed, even if courts in the final resort were to maintain their generous attitude, they might very well, as we have just seen, be paralysed as far as their remedial powers are concerned. This is a very good reason to send the responsibility for group rights to where it belongs: to the majority and its institutions, the judicial process being merely part of the ongoing dialectic process associated with democratic systems.

THE ASSERTION OF GROUP RIGHTS BY GROUPS

One of the characteristics of group rights is precisely that they are attributed to groups, for their benefit and protection. Of course, over and above their constitutionalised rights, groups exist within time and space and are sometimes located within a territory. Constitutional provisions and case law have taught us that the numerical importance of the group's membership may carry some important consequences, as for the sliding scale approach adopted by the Supreme Court of Canada in *Mahe*; inversely, numbers should not be relevant when individual rights are concerned. The geographical dimension of group rights might also be very important as is the case, for instance, as far as school restructuring along linguistic lines in Quebec, or aboriginal nations and peoples are concerned.

One of the crucial questions in this context becomes that of defining precisely the groups to whom a group right is attributed and, by way of consequence, which ones may benefit from the rights and its attributes flowing from the constitutionalisedright. In attempting to answer the question we find ourselves in a "Russian doll" situation where the group exists, sometimes with a "group within the group", and sometimes even with a "group within the group, within the group".

Which group in such situations has the legitimacy conferred by group rights, and how far does this legitimacy extend? There are no obvious solutions to such difficult questions as the recent discussions in Quebec around language advertising rights or aboriginal rights during the Charlottetown constitutional round show. Nevertheless, a Human Rights Committee from the United Nations recently ruled about the question of Bill 178 in Quebec (about language advertising rights) that under section 27 of the International Covenant on Civil and Political Rights, the majoritarian frame of reference is, within a federal state, the whole state, and not one of its units such as a province in Canada. In this case the anglophone minority in Quebec was therefore not considered a minority group as such, which meant that it could not benefit from the protection of the Covenant[11].

What must be understood from such a ruling and from the type of problems raised by group rights, is that groups to whom groups rights are conferred must consequently possess rights which are necessary to the very meaning and purpose of these group rights. Over and above their contents, group rights therefore confer a legitimacy for the group to preserve and enhance its characteristics. This is especially true and relevant when the group possesses some form of territorial presence or jurisdiction. A necessary form of self-determination is intrinsically attached to the group right. It not only can, but must be asserted and exercised, otherwise the purpose of the group right might well be defeated. Such forms of self-determination are perfectly legitimate and must therefore at least be tolerated by the majority. The basic tolerance they require from the majority somehow does not seem to be part of the Canadian majoritarian culture, at least as far as linguistic or aboriginal rights are concerned.

The right of groups to assert some form of self-determination should not mean, of course, that everything can be done under the pretext of group rights, otherwise the majority rule would be more or less replaced by a minority rule. The question at this point is to identify how the conflicts can be resolved between the rights necessary to the minority group and the individual rights present.

As already mentioned, the starting point to approaching the interpretation of group rights lies in the adoption of a purposive approach. Indeed, such a purposive approach lies at the heart of the official interpretative approach of the Supreme Court and is in the spirit of the Vienna Draft of the United Nations. This purposive approach does not only apply to the operationalisation of group rights, but must also be used, logically, in conciliating the rights at issue in cases of conflict between group interests and individual rights. In such a context, the norms developed and applied by the group will gain their legitimacy — and their legality should then be recognised by the courts — as long as they flow logically from the group right and are necessary to protect the group's characteristics which form the very reason why the group's rights were grantedin the first place. In cases where a conflict emerges for a particular individual between the group's materialisation of a group right flowing from one of its characteristics and an individual right otherwise protected, the process for finding a solution then becomes easier to conceptualise. The balancing process familiar to other branches of constitutional law should then be adopted primarily because group rights cannot and should not be conceived in complete isolation of the context in which they are exercised. Such a confrontation process is of a particular importance because it essentially provides for the essence of the evolutionary process for group rights. The process ultimately establishes, at least within the judicial forum, a proper and more rational form of dialogue between groups, that is, between the majority and the minority groups involved, whoever forms the majority or the minority, the minority group or the minority group within the minority group.

As pointed out earlier, the judicial forum is not the only forum where such balancing of rights goes on in a democratic system taken globally where a dialogue must exist between the various elements and institutions of the State. It is, however, the ultimate forum where rights are arbitrated and, short of a constitutional amendment, where the results of an arbitration are in some respects final. In a majority of cases, the arbitration should therefore be accomplished primarily by the actors themselves and should be articulated in political terms, the group rights and individual rights being discussed for what they are and for what they mean. Such debates in truly democratic societies are never easy to have. They are sometimes particularly difficult for governments, as the recent advertising language debates in Quebec (Bill 178) demonstrate.

Short of agreement at this level of discussion, judicial arbitration merely becomes another forum of discussion. The characteristics of the judicial process obviously influence the way the debate will be conducted at this level: the discussion is of course about the essence of the rights in question, but will be articulated through the prism and, officially at least, a certain rationality of the law. The actors then have to explain and elaborate their points of view in a way and with a depth never required before. This rationalisation process is a most important form of dialogue in our democratic process. The resulting judicial decision will be fully justified and will represent the final word, not necessarily on the extent and the interpretation which must be given to the group or the individual right at issue but, rather, about the understanding of the result of a balancing process at this point in time. It will then become part of the record the actors will use to subsequently discuss and argue their respective rights, whether they are of a group, an individual or of a collective nature.

CONCLUSION

A dialectic approach to the interpretation and operationalisation of group rights should therefore be adopted. Under such an approach, group rights would be understood for what they are and what they are supposed to represent: a means, for a group to whom constitutional protection was, at a certain point in time at least, deemed important and necessary. Recent and not so recent political discussions demonstrate that group rights have been and still are misunderstood and mistrusted. Part of the explanation probably lies with the reflex of conferring an absolute nature to rights, and specially to individual rights. This discourse is in line with what thepolitical discourse of the early 1980's wanted Canadians to believe and it was only one of the great Trudeauist deceptions of that era. Nothing should be less true than the "sanctity" of individual rights; they are by no means absolute and s.1 of the *Charter* confirms, if need be, the relativity of individual rights and their articulation with the rights of the collectivity. Under such a dialectic approach, it is therefore important to get rid of the "absoluteness" approach of rights. It is submitted, as far as group rights are concerned that they are no less illegitimate, within our constitutional system, than s. 1 collective rights which are asserted and recognised by the courts everyday. In other words, group rights should be taken much more seriously than they are now by all the political actors.

In the context of group rights, flexibility and tolerance should be two essential values shared by all actors. The majority should be tolerant and open towards the group and its assertions of rights which are certainly as legitimate, as we have seen, as the individual or collective rights the majoritarian group claims to rely upon. But the group itself also has duties. The first one is to actively protect and develop its group rights and to actively exercise the self-determination aspects which flow from it. This would avoid situations such as those of francophone or aboriginal groups which have to claim the respect for their group rights which have been ignored for very long period of time. The second duty of the groups to whom rights are conferred is, reciprocally, to exercise their rights with all the necessary tolerance and understanding for its own minority (the minority within the minority), of course taking into account the necessity of protecting its own group rights.

In that context, the solutions are rarely clear and easy to identify or arbitrate. We should, I believe, steer clear from the notion that group rights are essentially different and of a lesser value from other types of rights within our constitutional system. They should be recognised and respected for what they are. Recent history shows that indeed, individual rights *per se* are often not sufficient within our society to grant a necessary constitutional protection to groups and individual members of such groups, whether they are linguistic or aboriginal. An ongoing political, and sometimes judicial, dialogue about the rights and interests in issue should always be the process to be favoured and cherished. I believe that Bill Lederman would have agreed with this approach.

NOTES

1. *Société des Acadiens v. Assn. of Parents*, [1986] 1 S.C.R. 549.
2. *Re Bill 107*, [1993] 2 S.C.R. 511.
3. *Mahe v. Alberta*, [1990] 1 S.C.R. 342.
4. TR/93-54, March 12, 1993, CAN. GAZ II, vol.127, no. 7, p.1588 (April 7, 1993). It reads:
    16.1(1) The English linguistic community and the French linguistic community in New Brunswick have equality of status and equal rights and privileges, including the right to distinct educational institutions and such distinct cultural institutions as are necessary for the preservation and promotion of those communities.

    (2) The role of the Legislature and Government of New Brunswick to preserve and promote the status, rights and privileges referred to in subsection (1) is affirmed.
5. HOGG, P., *Constitutional Law of Canada*, 3rd ed., p.144
6. *Re Manitoba Language Rights*, [1985] 1 S.C.R. 721.
7. *R. v. Mercure*, [1988] 1 S.C.R. 234; *R. v. Paquette* [1990] 2 S.C.R. 1103.
8. *Manitoba Public Schools Reference*, [1993] 1 S.C.R. 839.
9. *A.G. Quebec v. Blaikie*, [1979] 2 S.C.R. 1016; *A.G. Manitoba v. Forest*, [1979] 2 S.C.R. 1032.
10. *Min. Empl. & Immigr. v. Schachter*, [1992] 2 S.C.R. 679.
11. *McIntyre v. Gov. of Quebec United Nations Human Rights Ctee*, #CCPR/C/47/D/ 359/1989 and 385/1989, 5, April 1993.

Aboriginal Rights and the Constitution: A Story Within a Story?

Darlene Johnston

INTRODUCTION

I welcome this opportunity to participate in the Lederman Symposium. Although I never had the privilege of meeting Professor Lederman, I do appreciate his profound contribution to Canadian constitutional scholarship. His writings demonstrate both commitment to constitutional renewal and respect for social and historical context. These qualities are essential in understanding group rights, particularly the rights of aboriginal peoples.

Proponents of group rights generally point to section 35 of the Constitution as a prime example of legal rights being vested explicitly in groups. Section 35 declares that "the existing aboriginal and treaty rights of the aboriginal peoples of Canada are hereby recognized and affirmed."

In attributing constitutionally protected rights to peoples rather than to individuals, the framers of the *Constitution Act, 1982* seem to have moved ahead of the theoreticians. Legal and political philosophers are just beginning to debate such issues as whether groups have an existence or value independent of their members and whether rights can or should be vested in groups as opposed to being vested in individual members.

As this debate unfolds, courts are being asked to give concrete meaning to the newly entrenched guarantees. Group rights, however poorly understood, are a Canadian constitutional reality. They promise to pose a continuing constitutional dilemma.

As a proponent of group rights, I must confess my own faith in the value of community. I belong to the Saugeen Ojibway Nation. I come from a reserve called Neyaashiinigmiing, which translates into English as "point of land surrounded by water". My identity as an individual is inextricably linked to my participation in and commitment to this community. For me, it is a matter of intuition and experience that my community has value and that it needs protection from the group-destructive potential of the Canadian state. Whether my intuition can be grounded in a coherent theory of rights is another matter. I am not a philosopher. By training, I am a lawyer. Over the past few years, I have had the opportunity to test whether the courts can fulfil the promise of group protection contained in section 35. I think that the meaning of collective rights can best be explored by concrete example. In this paper, I propose to examine the leading case on section 35, *R v. Sparrow*[1], and its application to a fishing rights case involving my own community.

A STORY WITHIN A STORY

I would like to begin with a quotation from Michael McDonald, a professor of philosophy at the University of Waterloo. Professor McDonald is a strong proponent of group rights. He has been instrumental in developing a vocabulary for the emerging debate. In his article, "Should Communities Have Rights? Reflections on Liberal Individualism" , he discusses his vision of collective rights:

> With collective rights, a group is a rights-holder: hence, the group has standing in some larger moral context in which the group acts as a right-holder in relation to various duty-bearers or obligants. This is to say that for collective rights I picture a shared understanding within another shared understanding. First, there is the understanding that makes disparate individuals into a group or collective. Second, there is a larger or more encompassing society in which that group stands as a right-holder vis a vis others. So with minority rights, a minority, united by its group-constituting understanding, acts or tries to act as a rights-holder in a larger normative, social or legal, context. In particular, the minority wants its shared understanding recognized and respected as a distinct part of the larger social understanding in the society in which the minority is a part. To put this in terms of narratives, minority rights involve a story within a story. The stories are related but distinct. One story is not to be eliminated and replaced by the other. The options of assimilation and separation are ruled out as is the option of the substitution of one by the other.[2]

I would like to discuss whether Professor Mcdonald's metaphor of a story within a story is applicable to the situation of aboriginal peoples within the context of the Canadian state. Section 35 purports to secure a space for aboriginal stories within the larger framework of the Canadian constitution. I think there is a danger, in this postentrenchment era, to take section 35 for granted. Seen squarely within its historical context, section 35 represents a remarkable reversal of the group-destructive policy which the federal government had pursued for more than a century.

The history of the relationship between aboriginal peoples and the Canadian state is rife with attempts to eliminate the aboriginal story; to substitute the Euro-Canadian story; to deny that there was any story before 1492 and the arrival of Columbus. In the aboriginal story, we can recount direct attacks on the structural integrity of our communities. The practice of dispossession of traditional lands, the relocation to small, isolated, often barren reserves: these are all too-familiar episodes. We can point to institutionalized, even legalized, procedures designed to deconstruct aboriginal communities.

One of the most group-destructive practices was the legal procedure under the *Indian Act* known as enfranchisement. On its face, enfranchisement sounds like a good thing. If you start from the proposition that the right to vote is a good, and if you realize that before 1960, status Indians as defined under the *Indian Act* were denied the right to vote in federal elections, then a process designed to give Indians the vote must also constitute a good. However, enfranchisement was not intended to give "Indians" the vote but to turn them into non-Indians to avoid the legislativelysanctioned discrimination. Parliament presumed that it could convert Indians into nonIndian British subjects. In return for giving up their status, enfranchised individuals were able to vote in federal elections. Other incentives offered to the enfranchised included an allotment of reserve lands and a share of the tribes' assets. In a very real sense, enfranchisement involved the separation of the individual from the community.

To those who do not value community, the harm posed by enfranchisement may not be obvious. Elsewhere, I have tried to capture the impact of the procedure:

What did enfranchisement entail for a First Nations individual? At the most basic level, it required self-alienation. The power of the Canadian state to determine one's identity had to be accepted. The Creator's gift of identity as an aboriginal person had to be rejected — cast aside as inferior to that of a British colonial subject. Enfranchisement also involved a denial of community autonomy and rejection of the values that community membership represented. It meant standing outside the circle that contained one's ancestors, language, traditions, and spirituality. For what? To escape the humiliating disabilities that the Canadian state had imposed in the first place. To acquire a separate allotment of land, in contravention of the tradition of communal stewardship of land. To be able to alienate one's allotment, ignoring the needs of future generations. The statistics reveal that the hardships imposed by the Indian Act proved more tolerable than the renunciation of identity [and community] that enfranchisement involved.[3]

Aboriginal communities proved quite resistant to the threat posed by enfranchisement. Between Confederation and 1920 only 102 individuals became enfranchised.[4]

The lengths to which the government was prepared to go in promoting the disintegration of aboriginal communities was demonstrated in 1920 when the enfranchisement procedure became compulsory. The *Indian Act* was amended to give the Superintendent General of Indian Affairs the power to enfranchise individuals against their will. The author of the amendment was Duncan Campbell Scott. While testifying before a Commons Committee reviewing the proposed amendments, Scott defended compulsory enfranchisement:

> I want to get rid of the Indian problem. I do not think as a matter of fact, that this country ought to continuously protect a class of people who are able to stand alone. That is my whole point. I do not want to pass into the citizen's class people who are paupers. This is not the intention of the Bill. But after one hundred years, after being in close contact with civilization it is enervating to the individual or to a band to continue in a state of tutelage, when he or they are able to take their positions as British citizens or Canadian citizens, to support themselves, and stand alone. That has been the whole purpose of Indian education and advancement since the earliest times. One of the very earliest enactments was to provide for enfranchisement of the Indian. So it is written in our law that the Indian was eventually to become enfranchised.

> ...Our object is to continue until there is not a single Indian in Canada that hasnot been absorbed into the body politic, and there is no Indian question, and no Indian Department, that is the whole object of this Bill.[5]

If under Canadian law Indians were destined to be "absorbed", it can hardly be said that there was room for the aboriginal story within the Canadian story. It is clear that Mr. Scott did not value community. There was to be no middle ground between the individual and the state. Indians were to "stand alone".

Contrary to Professor McDonald's model, the intention was to eliminate one story and replace it with another. It may be tempting to dismiss Mr. Scott simply as a bureaucrat from an unenlightened era. Can the same be said of the architect of the *Charter*? In 1969, Prime Minister Trudeau showed the same impulse to replace the aboriginal story in defending his governments now infamous "White Paper":

> We can go on treating the Indians as having special status. We can go on adding bricks of discrimination around the ghetto in which they live and at the same time perhaps helping them preserve certain cultural traits and certain ancestral rights. Or we can say you're at a crossroads — the time is now to decide whether the Indians will be a race apart in Canada or whether it will be Canadians of full status. And this is a difficult choice. It must be a very agonizing choice to Indian peoples themselves because, on the one hand, they realize that if they come into society as total citizens

they will be equal under the law but they risk losing certain of their traditions, certain aspects of a culture and perhaps even certain of their basic rights.[6]

Mr. Trudeau had seriously underestimated the strength of attachment to culture and tradition which existed within aboriginal communities. The scheme to bring us into Canadian society as undifferentiated individuals, stripped of our collective rights, encountered massive resistance and was abandoned.

Little more than a decade later, Mr. Trudeau's patriated Constitution entrenched Indian special status and guaranteed equality before the law. Seen from the perspective of compulsory enfranchisement and the "White Paper", section 35 represents a dramatic reversal in the Canadian story about aboriginal peoples.

As a chapter in the repatriation story, section 35 demonstrates the extent to which actors can modify the script. It was initially conceived by the drafters of the Constitution as a non-derogation clause, to protect treaty rights from the levelling effect of the Charter's equality guarantees. A sustained aboriginal lobby managed to transform the shield into a sword. The extent of this transformation was not lost on the politicians. At the last moment, the aboriginal rights guarantee was deleted from the package in an effort by the federal negotiators to appease the concerns of the western premiers. Only a very strong public outcry, including the voice of prominent jurist Thomas Berger, managed to save section 35. However, the revived guarantee contained a substantial compromise. It spoke only to "existing" aboriginal and treaty rights. Although it represented more than a non-derogation clause, the final version could hardly be called a sword. At best, it provided a broader shield, designed to protect aboriginal rights not only from section 15 challenges by private parties but also from government infringement.

In spite of the eleventh-hour compromise, section 35 holds out a promise of accommodation. On its face, it has the potential to create a space for aboriginal peoples as aboriginal peoples within the Canadian constitution. Of course, the extent to which this potential can be realized depends largely upon the interpretation that section 35 receives from Canadian courts. The first interpretation provided by the Supreme Court of Canada has set the parameters for the aboriginal rights story within the Canadian constitutional saga.

THE *SPARROW* STORY

On May 25, 1984, Ron Sparrow went fishing for salmon. Mr. Sparrow is a member of the Musqueam Indian Band whose traditional territory includes the Fraser River estuary. Mr. Sparrow was fishing in waters covered by a licence issued to his Band by the Department of Fisheries and Oceans. He was charged under a provision of the *Fisheries Act* because the drift net he was using was longer than the restricted length specified in the licence. Mr. Sparrow did not deny that his net was longer than the licence allowed. However, he defended the charge by asserting that section 35 guaranteed his aboriginal right to fish and that the net length restriction was inconsistent with section 35 and therefore unenforceable.

Mr. Sparrow's case was heard by the British Columbia Provincial Court, then appealed to the County Court, then to the British Columbia Court of Appeal and finally to the Supreme Court of Canada. It provided the Supreme Court with the opportunity "to explore for the first time the scope of s.35(1) of the *Constitution Act, 1982*, and to indicate its strength as a promise to the aboriginal peoples of Canada."[7]

The Court heard from several interveners, including six provincial attorneys general, several commercial fishing organizations, and the Assembly of First Nations. It was presented with wildly differing views of the meaning behind the text that "existing" aboriginal rights are "recognized and affirmed". Some supporters of aboriginal rights argued that the multitude of rights that had been abrogated or extinguished by state action prior to 1982 could be revived by section 35. The government lawyers, by contrast, argued that "existing" means that section 35 only protects the exercise of rights in the manner by which they were regulated in 1982, the so-called "frozen rights" thesis.

On the issue of "existing" the Court chose a middle ground between revived and frozen rights. Only such rights as had survived unextinguished until 1982 could gain protection from section 35. However, once within the guarantee provided by section 35, the content of the right was not determined by the regulatory regime in place in 1982. The Court held that "the phrase "existing aboriginal rights" must be interpreted flexibly so as to permit their evolution over time."[8]

It was obvious to the Court that there would be competing perceptions of whether a given aboriginal right could be termed "existing". In an attempt to ensure that both the aboriginal and the government voices were heard, the Court developed a procedural framework which involved a series of shifting burdens of proof. Paradoxically, it provides an opportunity for the telling of aboriginal stories while preserving the state story of elimination.

At the outset of any section 35 litigation, whether criminal or civil, the onus is on the aboriginal claimant to establish the right for which constitutional protection is being sought. This evidentiary burden is really an invitation to aboriginal people to tell their own story. In *Sparrow*, courts are urged to stretch their imaginations beyond conventional legal categories in order to glimpse the aboriginal reality. The Supreme Court lead by example in its approach to the right claimed by Mr. Sparrow:

> Fishing rights are not traditional property rights. They are rights held by a collective and are in keeping with the culture and existence of that group. Courts must be

careful, then, to avoid the application of traditional common law concepts of property as they develop their understanding of ... the "sui generis" nature of aboriginal rights.

While it is impossible to give an easy definition of fishing rights, it is possible, and, indeed, crucial, to be sensitive to the aboriginal perspective itself on the meaning of the rights at stake.[9]

The Court is acknowledging that aboriginal peoples are in the best position to speak to the nature of our rights, of the role they have in our cultures and their importance to our continued existence as peoples.

Once we have had our say, the onus shifts to the Crown to prove extinguishment. Its hard to imagine any other rights litigation in which the government is formally encouraged to demonstrate that it has intentionally prohibited the exercise of an established right. As long as the extinguishment occurred before 1982, there is no requirement to justify the state interference with aboriginal or treaty rights.

Extinguishment of rights is a concept that Canadian law has reserved exclusively for aboriginal peoples. It is a tragic example of the divergence between legal reasoning and aboriginal reality. As a lawyer, I can recite the test for extinguishment, but as a descendant of leaders who negotiated several treaties with the Crown I cannot accept that treaty rights can exist and then cease to exist. Treaties are a matter of honour. The promises that the Crown has made do not disappear when the government chooses to violate them. What has been lost is the Crown's honour, not the rights that were secured by treaty.

Rather than speaking of extinguishment of rights, the Court should have acknowledged that it was limiting its ability to enforce the promises that the Crown has made to aboriginal peoples. The government is not accountable for having violated rights before 1982, provided its intention to do so was "clear and plain". The lastminute inclusion of the word "existing" has preserved the power of state story to displace the aboriginal story.

Only if the government fails to prove extinguishment does the promise of section 35 become operative. The courts will recognize only those rights which have not been thoroughly repressed as of 1982. Rights which manage to survive the extinguishment test are accorded constitutional recognition and affirmation.

On the meaning of "recognized and affirmed" the Court was presented with competing theories. Once again, it looked for middle ground. The Court was not prepared to protect surviving aboriginal rights from all forms of state interference. Since section 35 does not appear within the *Charter* portion of the *Constitution Act, 1982*, infringements cannot be justified by reference to section 1. However, the Court did not interpret the textual placement of section 35 as conferring absolute immunity from state regulation. It did provide some restraints on the government propensity for interference with aboriginal rights by establishing a test of justification.

The scope of the scrutiny is disturbingly uneven. Not all infringements require justification. Only those infringements which impose "undue hardship" have to be justified by the government. Apparently aboriginal people are expected to accept some hardship as our "due". It remains to be seen if the courts differ from the governments in their assessment of the degree of hardship which aboriginal people are owed.

At this point in the *Sparrow* story, an aboriginal listener will be bemused, if not disillusioned. Rights exist only if they haven't been absolutely violated; but existing rights are not absolute. Infringements of existing rights must meet a justificatory standard; unless, of course, the interference does not satisfy the prior standards of unreasonableness, adversity and undue hardship. The burden falls on the aboriginal claimant to establish a sufficiently adverse interference with a "protected" right before the government is required to justify its infringement.

This burden is misplaced. Once the aboriginal claimant has established an "existing" right, the protection of section 35 should be automatic. The courts should then call upon the Crown to demonstrate the reasonableness of its limitation. After all, Ron Sparrow proved that he had an existing aboriginal right to fish. He exercised that right and was charged for using a net longer than 25 fathoms. Before the Crown can secure a criminal conviction shouldn't it be required to prove that this net length restriction is reasonable and necessary? Why should the defendant have the additional burden of proving that this state interference is sufficiently adverse in order to trigger the protection of section 35?

This stage of the *Sparrow* analysis, the test for "prima facie interference with an existing aboriginal right", is partially redeemed by the Supreme Court's attention to specificity. "The inquiry with respect to interference begins with a reference to the characteristics or incidents of the right at stake."[10] Once again, the Court has created a space for the telling of the aboriginal story. Despite the inappropriateness of the preconditions to the justification analysis, these can typically be satisfied by the aboriginal claimant. There is no shortage of evidence that government regulation of aboriginal rights are unreasonable and create adversity.

If this last hurdle is cleared by the aboriginal claimant, then the protection of section 35 comes into play. The courts assume their conventional constitutional role of scrutinizing the impugned regulation for a "valid legislative objective". However, the *Sparrow* analysis adds a "guiding interpretive principle" which is unique to section 35. The Supreme Court recognizes that "the honour of the Crown is at stake in dealing with aboriginal peoples. The special trust relationship and the responsibility of the government vis-à-vis aboriginals must be the first consideration in determining whether the legislation or action in question can be justified."[11]

The history of this special trust relationship is a story that the governments have been keen to forget. In reminding the Crown of its obligation to respect aboriginal and treaty rights, the Court has lent its constitutional weight to the voice of aboriginal peoples. Although section 35 was not interpreted as the all-encompassing, resuscitative force that aboriginal peoples had been awaiting, it does provide a little space for aboriginal stories within the context of the Canadian constitutional story. Just how much space is the task of intrepid storytellers to discover.

THE STORY OF JONES AND NADJIWON

The opportunity to tell a story within a story poses a dilemma for some aboriginal peoples. There are those who feel that it is not appropriate to tell their nation's story within the confines of the Canadian constitutional story. Many do not regard the *Canada Act, 1982* as an appropriate vessel for their rights. Still more do not trust the Canadian courts to adequately protect those rights. Already, revered elders have had their sacred stories dismissed as not being grounded in reality, as judicially perceived.[12]

In my community, many were skeptical of the promise contained in section 35. However, we did not have the choice of whether or not to go to court. In 1989, our chief, Howard Jones, and members of a well-known fishing family, Francis and Marshall Nadjiwon, were charged with taking more lake trout than permitted by the commercial fishing licence issued to our band by the Ministry of Natural Resources. Faced with potential fines and jail terms, the chief and fishermen were advised to defend the charges by challenging the constitutional validity of the government-imposed limit on our community harvest of lake trout.

My people, the Saugeen Ojibway, are a fishing people. It is no accident that our traditional territory is surrounded by water. For thousands of years we have occupied the peninsula which separates Lake Huron and Georgian Bay. Today it is commonly known as the Bruce Peninsula, but we continue to call it the Saugeen Peninsula. The peninsula is not hospitable to farmers. Our people survived by fishing, hunting and gathering.

In the last century, our leaders had to make some very difficult choices in the face of encroachments by squatters and the failure of the Crown to live up to its promises to protect our lands. Between 1836 and 1854, the Saugeen Territory was reduced from a 2 million acre tract to a cluster of small reserves along the shore of Lake Huron and Georgian Bay. The location of these reserves, adjacent to the best fishing grounds within our once vast Territory, attests to the importance of the fishery to our way of life. In an effort to ensure our survival as a people, our leaders made deliberate decisions to tie our destiny to the fishery.

In 1836, our chiefs signed a treaty which surrendered 1.5 million acres in return for a promise by the Lieutenant Governor that "he would remove all the white people who were in the habit of fishing on their grounds." Although several subsequent treaties were signed involving lands, our fishing rights were never surrendered. When faced with criminal prosecution for exercising our fishing rights, the defence was grounded in this promise from 1836.

Although section 35 provided an opportunity to tell the Saugeen Ojibway story, a great deal depends upon the listener. As someone who stands outside the community, there is a risk that the judge will devalue what is experienced as essential to those within. To our great relief, we perceived that Judge Fairgrieve was a good listener. He seemed genuinely interested in our story. He allowed more than 400 exhibits to be introduced documenting our history as a fishing people. The trial was held in a courtroom some two hours from the reserve. To facilitate the testimony of elders, however, the trial judge travelled to Cape Croker. By visiting the reserve, he gained both cultural and geographical context for our fishing rights. Judge Fairgrieve took seriously the Supreme Court's admonition "to be sensitive to the aboriginal perspective itself on the meaning of the rights at stake."

From the Saugeen Ojibway perspective, our people have lived by fishing for thousands of years. To live by fishing means more than to fish for our own consumption. There are also spiritual, cultural and commercial aspects to the fishery. In earlier times, we traded fish for corn and other necessities. Today, our fishermen sell to commercial buyers to earn income to support their families. One example of the fishery's cultural importance is the significantly greater retention of our language among families engaged in traditional fishing activity.

Perhaps the most distinctive aspect of our understanding of our right to fish is that it belongs to the community, not to the individual. The government's licensing regime, introduced in the 1850's, respected this reality by issuing community licences in the name of the chiefs. When fees were eventually imposed for issuing licences, the expense was borne by the community, not by individual fishermen.

Dr. Roz Vanderburgh, an anthropologist who studied traditional resource use at Cape Croker interviewed several elders during the mid-1970's. As an expert witness at trial she was asked if the fishery was seen as a collective right as opposed to an individual resource. She replied: "It never occurred to me to even ask that question because it is so clear that there is no sense of individual ownership of any of the natural resources by aboriginal peoples, not just the people at Cape Croker, but by any of the aboriginal peoples that I've worked with."

Judge Fairgrieve was persuaded by the evidence introduced to support the Saugeen Ojibway understanding of the rights at stake. On the issue of whether there is an existing aboriginal or treaty right to fish for commercial purposes, he found that "the Saugeen have a collective ancestral right to fish for sustenance purposes in their traditional fishing grounds...It is the band's continuing communal right to continue deriving "sustenance" from the fishery resource which has always been an essential part of the community's economic base."[13]

Having found an existing commercial fishing right, the trial judge had to determine whether the lake trout quota, which the fishermen had been charged for exceeding, constituted an infringement. The lake trout quota had been imposed by the Ministry of Natural Resources in 1984 as part of its overall program to "rationalize" the commercial fishery in the Great Lakes. Without consulting with our people, the Ministry decided that lake trout should not be a commercial species and restricted its harvest by labelling lake trout as "incidental catch". This meant that fishermen were expected to target other "commercial" species for harvest such as whitefish. If, incidentally, they caught lake trout in their nets while trying to catch whitefish, they could sell only the amount specified in the licence. The problem is that the labels created by the Ministry bear no relation to the habits of fish. Whitefish and lake trout don't realize that one is a "commercial" species and the other "incidental". They swim in the same waters and get caught in the same nets.

Similarly, the quotas imposed on our people bore no relation to our community harvest. Before the imposition of the quota system, our fishermen caught and sold more lake trout than whitefish. This predominance of lake trout was due, in part, to an aggressive stocking program undertaken by the Ministry in Georgian Bay. Yet, when the Ministry imposed its quotas, our community was limited to harvesting 10,022 pounds of lake trout and 18,200 pounds of whitefish. At the time, lake trout was selling for two dollars per pound, limiting the community harvest to a value of $20,044. This quota was too low to sustain even one individual operation, let alone the more than fifteen families who were dependent on the lake trout fishery for their livelihood.

The ratio of the lake trout to the whitefish quota made a bad situation worse. The limit on lake trout would always be reached before the allowable harvest of whitefish. To continue fishing for whitefish meant catching lake trout which could not be sold. The fishermen were faced with a dilemma. They could continue fishing, and simply dump "incidental" fish, a practice common among non-native commercial fishermen. This waste was disrespectful to the fish and the resulting pollution disrespectful to the water. To avoid this wrongful conduct, they could pull their nets and stop fishing, but then they were at a loss as to how to provide for their families. Alternatively, they could continue fishing and selling, conduct which the Ministry had made illegal by imposing a limit which took no account of the existing communal rights.

In the eyes of the fishermen, the last option was the most justifiable, believing as they did in their right to fish as their fathers and grandfathers had taught them. The Ministry had enforcement officers to enforce its view of what harvest our community was entitled to, and so our chief and fishermen were charged.

Before the Ministry was required to justify the imposition of the lake trout quota, we had to prove that this "interference" amounted to an "infringement" of our now judicially-recognized communal right. The trial judge, in his reasons, expressed some uneasiness with this stage of the *Sparrow* analysis. On the aboriginal burden of characterizing the interference as unreasonable or unnecessary he observed: "All of these questions might have appeared more relevant to the question of whether the interference was justified, not whether any interference occurred."[14]

In regarding the distinction between interference and infringement as somewhat artificial, Judge Fairgrieve was in good company. The Ontario Court of Appeal had already virtually collapsed the distinction. In *R.v. Bombay*, the first Ontario appellate decision to apply the *Sparrow* framework to treaty, as distinguished from aboriginal rights, concluded that "if interference is established, that will constitute a *prima facie* infringement of s.35(1)."[15]

Not surprisingly, the chief and fishermen had little difficulty establishing that the lake trout quota interfered with the exercise of our collective fishing rights. The trial judge made the following findings:

> In the context of the Cape Croker Band's right to fish commercially, there can be little doubt that the limit on the number of lake trout they could lawfully catch imposed an "adverse restriction" on the exercise of their right. The band's quota had already been reached by the end of June, only part way through the fishing season, and had the direct consequence of terminating the exercise of their right in relation to the species the band preferred to harvest. The restrictions clearly limited the income which the band members would have received had they been permitted to continue harvesting for splake [lake trout].

> In terms of assessing whether the quota caused "undue hardship", it is difficult to know what degree of hardship was "due" and to isolate the impact of the lake trout quota from other restrictions imposed as part of the same regulatory scheme. The financial hardship caused to the band by the curtailed commercial activity, however, was documented by the evidence. The band's fishing income is a crucial part of what was essentially a subsistence economy. More limited access to the resource caused by the quota produced greater deprivation and, predictably, contributed to

the negative consequences of increased unemployment and poverty on both an individual and communal level.[16]

This finding of communal hardship flows from the collective nature of the right at stake. The trial judge showed equal sensitivity to the aboriginal perspective on the meaning of the interference as well as the right.

The aboriginal task of establishing the right and the interference, though an evidentiary burden, is also a benefit. It is a rare opportunity to have an aboriginal story validated by an outsider in a position of authority. Of course, much depends upon the listener. After years of having protests fall on deaf ears, our elders and fishermen were relieved to have the trial judge listen respectfully. It was even more gratifying, perhaps, to see the Ministry of Natural Resources officials called upon to justify their interference with the exercise of our fishing rights.

As the first step in the justification analysis, *Sparrow* requires a valid legislative objective for the impugned regulation. The Ministry argued that the imposition of the lake trout quota was aimed at reducing mortality rates and establishing a selfsustaining lake trout population. *Sparrow* had already endorsed the validity of the conservation objective, suggesting that the "justification of conservation and resource management ... is surely uncontroversial."[17] *Sparrow* does not simply ask "why", but "how".

It is not enough for the Ministry to justify its interference by relying on stock assessment data and population models to establish the effects of quotas on mortality rates. The issue is not purely scientific. It is a matter of obligation. *Sparrow* requires the government to satisfy a second level of the justification test. Some things bear repeating:

> If a valid legislative objective is found, the analysis proceeds to the second part of the justification issue. Here, we refer back to the guiding interpretive principle derived from *Taylor* and *Guerin*. That is, the honour of the Crown is at stake in dealings with aboriginal peoples. The special trust relationship and the responsibility of the government vis-à-vis aboriginals must be the first consideration in determining whether the legislation or action in question can be justified.[18]

However well-meaning the Ministry's attempts to rehabilitate lake trout stocks, the method adopted had to honour earlier promises made by the Crown to our people.

If harvest controls are necessary to sustain the lake trout population, then allocations among competing users cannot be avoided. The allocations must be constitutional. Section 35, according to *Sparrow*, "demands that there be a link between the question of justification and the allocation of priorities in the fishery."[19] In *Sparrow*, the Supreme Court assigned a priority to the Musqueam food fishery which was second only to conservation. This did not mean that conservation could be practiced solely at the expense of the Indian food fishery . The Court explained:

> The significance of giving the aboriginal right to fish for food top priority can be described as follows. If, in a given year, conservation needs required a reduction in the number of fish to be caught such that the number equalled the number required for food by the Indians, then all the fish available after conservation would go to the Indians according to the constitutional nature of their fishing right. If more realistically, there were still fish after the Indian food fishing requirements were met, then the brunt of conservation measures would be borne by the practices of sport fishing and commercial fishing.[20]

Sparrow does not explicitly rank the priority to be accorded to treaty commercial fishing rights, this was the task which fell to Judge Fairgrieve.

Having found an existing collective right to fish for livelihood purposes and *prima facie* interference, the protection of section 35 had come into play. The promise of constitutional recognition and affirmation would mean little if the full right, including its commercial aspect, was not given priority. The trial judge ruled that the priority assigned to "Indian fishing" generally can include treaty commercial fishing where the particular facts establish the existence of such a fishery. "If it did not, it would be difficult to see any sense in which it had special constitutional status."[21]

The Ministry did not introduce any evidence that the treaty commercial fishery had received priority in the lake trout allocation. In fact, the opposite was established to the satisfaction of the trial judge:

> I accept that a consequence of the constitutional recognition and affirmation given by s.35(1) to the defendants' aboriginal and treaty rights to fish for commercial purposes is that the Saugeen Ojibway Nation has priority over other user groups in the allocation of surplus fishery resources, once the needs of conservation have been met. I am also satisfied that the evidence relating to the allocation of the quotas under the existing regulatory scheme has made no attempt to extend priority to the defendants' band. Scrutiny of the government's conservation plan discloses that anglers and non-native commercial fishermen have in fact been favoured, and that the allocation of quotas to the Chippewas of Nawash, much less the Saugeen Ojibway as a whole, did not reflect any recognition of their constitutional entitlement.

. . . . . .

While the allocation process adopted when the quota system was introduced in 1984 may have reflected social and political realities at the time, it is not at all apparent that the constitutional realities played any role at all. Neither has it been demonstrated that since that time appropriate adjustments have been made in response to a belated recognition of the priority of the band's right.[22]

In order to conserve a scarce resource, choices have to be made. Section 35 has introduced some constraints on the choices that the government can make. This new constitutional reality was brought home to the Ministry of Natural Resources when Judge Fairgrieve ruled that the requisite justification had not been provided and that, as a consequence, the lake trout quota imposed on the native fishery was of no force and effect.

THE END OF THE STORY, AND THE BEGINNING

In his concluding remarks, Judge Fairgrieve affirmed that section 35 had introduced a new chapter in the story of the relationship between aboriginal peoples and the Crown:

> ...a high-handed and adversarial stance on the part of the Ministry will neither meet the constitutional requirements with which, one would expect, it would consider itself duty-bound to comply, nor will it provide an enforceable regulatory scheme capable of achieving the conservation goals which it seeks. It is self-evident, I think, that s.35(1) of the *Constitution Act, 1982*, particularly after the judgment of the Supreme Court of Canada in *Sparrow*, dictated that a new approach be taken by the government to ensure that its policies discharge the obligations assumed by its constitutional agreement. I do not think it was ever suggested that there would necessarily be no adjustments required or no costs attached.[23]

Perhaps the biggest adjustment required is one of attitude. Many government officials have to unlearn the attitudes fostered by the old stories of assimilation and substitution. In providing constitutional protection for treaty and aboriginal rights, albeit protection that is limited and uneven, section 35 has created a space for aboriginal stories within the Canadian constitutional story.

NOTES

1. [1990] 1 S.C.R. 1075, 70 D.L.R. (4th) 385.
2. (1991) Canadian Journal of Law and Jurisprudence 217 at 220.
3. "First Nations and Canadian Citizenship" in W. Kaplan, ed., *Belonging: The Meaning and Future of Canadian Citizenship* (Montreal & Kingston: McGillQueen's University Press, 1993) 349 at 361-362.
4. Canada, Parliament, *Annual Report 1921*, Sessional Paper No.27, 13.
5. National Archives of Canada, RG 10, vol. 6810, file 470-2-3, vol.7: Evidence of D.C. Scott to the Special Committee of the House of Commons examining the Indian Act amendments of 1920.

6. P.E. Trudeau, excerpts from a speech given 8 August 1969, in Vancouver, as repro-
    duced in Cumming and Mickenberg, eds., *Native Rights in Canada*, 2nd ed. (Toronto:
    Indian-Eskimo Association of Canada, 1972), 331.
7. *Supra*, note 1.
8. *Ibid.*
9. *bid*, at p.1111.
10. *Ibid.*
11. *Ibid*, at p.1114 .
12. See *Delgamuukw v. British Columbia* (1991) 79 D.L.R (4th) 185 (B.C.S.C.)
13. *R. v. Jones et al* (1993), 14 O.R. (3d) 421 at 441.
14. *Ibid*, at 442.
15. *R. v. Bombay* [1993] 1 C.N.L.R. 92.
16. *Supra*, note 13 at p.442.
17. *Supra*, note 1 at 1113.
18. *Ibid*, at p.1114.
19. *Ibid*, at p.1115.
20. *Ibid*, at p.1116.
21. *Supra*, note 13 at 445.
22. *Ibid*, at p.449.
23. *Ibid*, at p.452-453.

Part Seven

JUDICIAL INDEPENDENCE AND RESPONSIBILITY

Unification of the Court System

Ian Scott[1]

I would like to congratulate all of you for turning out at this early hour to hear what I might have to say on what is a rather dry topic. I first got to know Bill Lederman when he was retained to argue a part of the brief in the Anti-Inflation case and we worked hard together on that brief. What we learned through that exercise is that for all his enormous talents and his great humanity, Bill Lederman was not an advocate. It was not that he was unpersuasive, because he was persuasive. It was not that he was not supremely intelligent, because he was. It was that he simply was incapable of saying something to which he was not totally, intellectually committed. That may have suited him perfectly as it did in a host of other careers, but it made him, at the end of the day, unsuited to the nefarious kind of work to which I have devoted my life.

I then came to know him when I came here as a student and teacher. One of the memories I have was Bill and Stuart Ryan, at the peak of their careers, spending all of their time in the Faculty Room having coffee, it seemed, for at least 8 hours a day. I had the opportunity to sit and listen to them and it was a rewarding experience. Two more civilized and interesting people than Stuart Ryan and Bill Lederman are hard to imagine. I am flattered see that Professor Ryan is here this morning.

I am very pleased to have been asked to participate in this symposium though I am not blessed with the most interesting of the various topics. The subject assigned to me is to try to plumb the connection and interaction between proposals for court structural change and the legitimate needs of an independent judiciary. I am in the course of preparing a paper and what I say this morning is preliminary only; it is designed to get the reaction of the Regional Senior Judge of Metropolitan Toronto before I commit the final text to print. I hasten to add that what I say is entirely a personal reflection based on something in excess of thirty years practising almost exclusively in the Ontario courts and a short or long period as Attorney General of Ontario, depending on your perspective. The subject I divide roughly into three sections. First of all some observations, highly preliminary and fragmentary about what judicial independence, properly understood, may require from our judicial trial structures and from attempts to redesign them. Secondly, something of the history of the structural change in our generation, especially trial court unification. Thirdly, a bare list, that cannot be more in the time allocated to me, of the pressure points, legitimate and illegitimate, where the demands of independence and trial court restructuring or unification interact. So let me begin.

As we address the subject consideration has to be given to what the important core values are that we as a community seek to preserve and protect by our notion of judicial independence. I would not have used the term "core values" except that George Thomson is here and he uses it a lot so I did want to get it in. Some of the core values are substantive and some of them are process focused. I have prepared just a rough list of what, in my view, those core values are that are at stake when we talk about judicial independence.

Now the good news from my point of view is that while Bill Lederman wrote a lot about judicial independence he did not write very much as far as I know about court restructuring, it being a phenomena that occurred rather late in his career. Therefore, unlike the other speakers in the program, I probably don't have Bill's spirit looking over my shoulder to criticize what I say, which is lucky. But I am conscious on the other hand that the list of core values that I would enunciate is probably narrower, indeed, I think, is narrower than the one that Professor Lederman would have proposed. However, the first substantive component that is designed to be protected by the notion of judicial independence, it seems to me, is the prerogative of the court to judicially review. It has to be conceded, whether the judiciary be regarded as the third branch of the government or not, under our Constitution and particularly in light of the Charter, that the court has a judicial review power that cannot be and should not be restrained, except as government sees fit to restrain it by whatever kinds of privative clauses may be designed by politicians to make their will effective. Judicial review is not only appropriate in a federal system, but it is also a requirement of a system that has an entrenched Charter. So, any court restructuring or any exercise trammelling the judicial review capacity of judges, I would regard as a fundamental interference with their independence that could not be tolerated.

The second component is that in order to make the capacity of the judiciary effective, it is necessary that sufficient resources be provided by the tax payer to enable the judiciary to perform its work in a modest and reasonable way. The allocation of resources in this area has to take two considerations into account. First, the legitimate needs of the judiciary to do their judicial review work and the other work of the court which is necessary but which is probably not constitutionally protected. The provision of resources by the taxpayer also has to take account of the total resource availability of the community and the other demands upon it. It is not simply a politician's folly to try and measure the health care system against the needs of the judiciary. Both needs are legitimate; neither has any particular primacy. The resource requirements of the judiciary, like the resource requirements of the health care system, have to be measured against not only the intrinsic value of the exercise being performed but also against the resource base of the community.

The third core value behind judicial independence is the preservation of the capacity to hear and decide cases freely, according to judicial values and with some modest limitations that I won't bore you with according to rules judicially devised. The fourth core value is a kind of institutional tenure system that insulates the institution of the judiciary and the individuals who compose it from other pressures to decide or not to decide.

I would list those four as the essential core values protected by the notion of judicial independence. It is a narrow list and I advance it cautiously recognizing that some here may find it uncomfortably narrow. I draw confidence only from a recent issue of the Lawyers Weekly in which the present Chief Justice of Canada is reported as saying that none of us should trivialize judicial independence and its importance by assigning it to cases to which it is clearly inappropriate. The journalist thought that the Chief Justice was making an oblique reference to those who thought that government sponsored gender sensitivity courses for judges were offensive to the notion of judicial independence. Whatever the Chief Justice may have been directing his mind to, the point he was making, it seems to me, was driven home perfectly on the facing page of the Lawyers Weekly which reported that the Quebec Superior Court had decided that parking charges for judges at the Quebec Court House were unconstitutional because they offended the principle of judicial independence. So my narrow list, I assert, has the imprimatur if not the Quebec Superior Court much more importantly the imprimatur, by implication at least, of the Chief Justice of Canada.

I select the narrow because I think another important value is the democratic majoritarian principle with which, quite appropriately, judicial independence will often collide. I began to think as I was working on this that if one principle had to give way to the other, where would I find myself? I decided to simply ignore that prospect and to assert that both principles must live together in total harmony at all times, but the majoritarian principle which asserts that free people have the right freely to make choices about how they will live is an important principle which leads me to reduce the list of core values assigned to judicial independence more than some might do.

Let me turn to the second part of my proposed paper which is some observations about trial restructuring in Canada. As Professor Barr has pointed out in a paper to which I will come, and again I am flattered and somewhat intimidated by his presence this morning, the process of trial restructuring is relatively new in this country — in the sense that for almost one hundred years, perhaps longer certainly in Ontario in the hundred years since the fundamental changes made by Sir Oliver Mowat in the last part of the last century — and the court system as we know it has remained, with minor modifications at the fringes, virtually intact. The senior court originally contemplated under s. 96 of the Constitution was relatively small, focused in one centre, Toronto in our case, and at intervals, holding assizes in various other places in the province, the court dealing expertly with a relatively confined number of major civil and criminal cases. Below the senior court was a county or district system that was focused on individual counties and districts with resident judges, highly decentralized, dealing early in the game with smaller civil and criminal cases but increasing its jurisdiction over a period of time to a level that was almost concurrent with the senior s. 96 court . The third level, historically in Ontario was a magistrate's or justice of the peace court system that was local, often part time and staffed by lay persons dealing with an enormous volume of criminal and civil matters. If you want to see for example what the Ontario magistrate and JP system probably looked like before the war you can go to Newfoundland where it remains preserved not in every aspect but is certainly intact. It remains a system highly infused with lay judges, highly informal in many ways and very local.

That was the system we lived with more or less for essentially a hundred years. The changes that occurred in the system as pressures of work and the demands of the community developed, were essentially changes that led to the expansion of one bench or the other as needs dictated or conversely to pushing of work down the system as increasing volumes developed. For example, the senior s. 96 court, confronted by enormous workloads, pressed for the district court to get concurrent jurisdiction and did what it could to push some of the case load down to that court. The senior court was not trying to evade the work; it was simply attempting to manage it effectively. But until the late 60's, there was no thought in this country, though there was in the United States, of restructuring the system. Now, as Professor Barr points out in his book, we have had an orgy of restructuring in Ontario and in Canada long before the Liberal government and the Attorney General of the day came along to make everything terrible. What we have done in Canada is essentially to merge the two s. 96 courts. By 1985, that merger had taken place in all but three provinces, Ontario, Nova Scotia and British Columbia. (Quebec's court system is rather different.) So merger was under way and had largely taken place by 1985.

In addition, the transformation of the local magistrates' courts from an informal mechanism to a highly professional province-wide system had begun and was, if not complete, certainly well underway by the early 1980's. And a major, significant and useful undertaking it was too. In this province it is much to the credit of previous Conservative governments that it was done.

Another fundamental restructuring that had begun, somewhat inconsistent with the other two methods of restructuring, was the creation from time to time and from place to place of specialized courts, usually in family law, designed to bring together the jurisdictional strains of family law in a court or a division of a court that would be assigned exclusively to deal with it. That process was underway across Canada. Merger had not occurred in Ontario but it was thought by everybody to be inevitable. Merger in a province this size bespoke a kind of regionalization and it fell to this Attorney General and our government to do what we thought was inevitable. So along with British Columbia and Nova Scotia, we brought merger to this province. It didn't seem to do much for my career but that was what was known as phase one of court reform and Ontario, instead of being aggressively radical or in the vanguard, was simply reflecting changes that were already completed elsewhere in the country or which were about to take place. If we had not participated we would have been the only province in the country with an unmerged court.

The second part of our court structuring reform was more radical: it was to build on the proposals made in the United States leading to a single unified trial court. What was contemplated here very simply was a court in which all the judges would have equivalent power and authority and in which all the judges would have capacity to decide the complete range of cases. This proposal did not necessarily require that each day they would be involved in deciding cases from the complete range. Indeed, it was explicitly contemplated that the judges would be allowed to reflect their own interests as well as the requirements of their chief justice in specializing in family, civil law or criminal law, as the needs of the community or their interests from time to time dictated. What was envisaged was a single trial court province-wide, decentralized on a regional basis, in which all the judges would have equal authority potentially to decide the complete range of cases. It was based on a model proposed early in the century by Dean Roscoe Pound at Harvard and adopted by the American Bar Association as its model of court structuring. It had been adopted by a number of states in the United States. The model appears in so many guises and varieties that to say it has been "adopted" is debatable, but I think it can be said that a single trial court of some type has been adopted in, I think Professor Barr says that last count, eleven or twelve American jurisdictions. The pre-eminent one of course is Illinois, where a single trial court has existed since the mid 70's, and where a single judge of the court has the capacity to try the most trivial small claims case, a criminal prosecution or a multi-million dollar civil suit.

So there is experience with the model in its various forms in the United States. Shortly after our proposal was made the Law Reform Commission of Canada, now extinct like the Attorney General for our respective sins, opted for a single trial court of Canada on the criminal side. That proposal in Canada created a fire storm no doubt because of the untypically aggressive way in which I advanced it, but I think also because it was perceived as striking at values which the judiciary held very deeply and which it thought in some cases were endangered by the proposal. Interestingly enough once the proposal was made a number of studies were commissioned. I had the impression they were commissioned to defeat the proposal. However, the Judicial Council of Canada commissioned a study in which Professor Barr looked at three unified trial courts in the United States. Putting aside all the rhetoric to look at what actually happened, I recall that he examined Illinois, South Dakota and one mid-western state, possibly Minnesota. The interesting thing was that — and this isn't usually Professor Barr's way, but there was something for everybody in that report, and I came away from reading it thinking that we were not wrong — the report suggests that the single trial court is in fact the wave of the future and that the conclusions that Professor Barr had drawn sustain the proposition rather than significantly modifying it. In any event, the proposed unified criminal trial court seems at present to be a dead letter.

Now I have to sum up briefly and what I want to do is simply to comment on a number of interactions between those proposals and the core values that I have identified associated with judicial independence. The attacks made on the proposals one has to identify as — to paraphrase the Chief Justice of Canada — either serious or trivial. There were some which in the light of history I am prepared to consign to the trivial list. First, there were complaints that it was an invasion of judicial independence to add more work for the judges or to subtract from the work they had. Depending on where you sit, you could take either one of those positions. It was thought by some that it was an invasion of judicial independence to make requirements of judges that were not extant at the time their patents were issued. It was claimed by some members of the courts that it was an invasion of independence to require judges who had not been required to travel, to travel, or interestingly enough, to deprive judges who had been accustomed to travelling, of the right to travel. With the greatest respect, I consign these interesting practical questions about whether the regime proposed was useful to the trivial and insignificant list from the perspective of the impact on judicial independence.

Nevertheless, there were some important issues that began to develop around the interaction with independence. The first was the role of the Chief Justice in any new structured system. In the district court system, judges did not need a

Chief Justice and would not have tolerated one in a practical sense because each judge was his or her own man or woman in a county or town and the judge ran the court. That was it. So the notion of a Chief Justice was for the district court a foreign one. Some one in Toronto filled in the gaps in the system but did not give day to day direction and assignment of work. By contrast, in the senior Superior Court, we have had some Chief Justices who have been enormously effective historically because of their personality, and others who have been less obvious in effectiveness. By and large, the court was operated by a collective sense of how the work should be done and how it should be assigned. Obviously, in a merged system in which the court was going to be expanded, that would no longer be a viable method of proceeding.

So the Courts of Justice Act, by virtue of s. 14 and its application at the provincial level, creates a Chief Justice for the first time in Ontario with real power, and a regional senior judge acting in the place of the Chief Justice in his or her region who has real power and power to direct and supervise the sittings — that is the wording of the section — and to make decisions respecting the assignment of judicial duties. S. 14 is, in a sense, looking at judicial independence from the judicial perspective and is a significant, though I think not a hotly contested, invasion of that independence. Connected with it, of course, is the importance of getting "judge-bureaucrats" to become Chief Justices who have ability to do the work and who are effective at it. It will not in every case be easy to do; there were discussions at the time that bear on the same subject about whether the Chief Justice should be appointed for life, as the federal government thought, and whether regional senior judges should be appointed for life or until they collapsed, also as the federal government thought. Alternatively, the province of Ontario thought and applied in its system, that such judges should be appointed for non-renewable terms of office. The whole notion of the Chief Justice as a real administrator and bureaucratic actor came to Ontario basically in the Courts of Justice Act. It was already well known in the United States when it came to Canada in that process.

The second change, the most hotly debated of all and my particular baby, were the provisions in sections 73 and 75 of the Act which created essentially regional management advisory committees. These committees were composed of the public service managers of the court system — the judges, the Crown Attorneys, the private bar and the public, or representatives of the public. Their function, as it was envisaged by the Minister at least, was to meet regularly to assess how the system was working and to make recommendations, not to make changes, but to make recommendations for change about the way the system was operating. The purpose was really twofold: first, to bring together in a setting on a regular basis all the legal actors, the Crown Attorneys who deliver mammoth amounts of work to the system, the lawyers defending, who have particular needs in how the system operates, and the judges of course, who run the system in large measure; and second, to discuss in a regular forum, among themselves, dare I say, as equal participants in the system, about how it might be better operated. In addition, we had the novel notion — everybody else does it across the world except we Canadians — that it might be possible in the late 80's to invite some lay people into that exercise and that they might actually have something to say. Lay people play major roles in running hospitals, educational institutions and the whole raft of institutions that the taxpayer funds but are remote from the judicial system. So that was our proposal and it created a lot of debate. It was watered down, as all my proposals were, into a satisfactory form, passed by the legislature and as far as I am concerned the committees have never been heard of since. I went out of office in 1990. I hope the people were appointed to them. I have never heard of anybody going to a meeting and I have never heard of anybody who has heard of anybody going to a meeting. So, maybe a Mike Harris government will bring the whole thing back. I thought that was a way of opening up an elite system that would be in the best sense liberal and in the best sense progressive.

There are two other areas which were of more immediate practical importance than our more visionary exercise. It is hard to think of it as visionary exercise, but I guess it was. First of all, the management of court staff. Who is going to manage them? To understand the problem here you have to understand the background, that the senior court staff had been the registrars and sheriffs. They were not professionals from the Ontario public service, but were by and large political appointments. Some were lawyers tired of their work; many were highly experienced political campaign managers including, in the case of Ottawa I think, Claude Bennett's barber who became the sheriff. They were in many cases excellent people who became excellent administrators and I am not being cynical, but they had little or no connection with the court system when they went into the job. They came into office in a county court house because that was the place of work, whether in Toronto or Brockville or Kingston, and they were taught by the local judge all they needed to know about the court system. Now they may have been taught things that were highly idiosyncratic, but that didn't matter — they were taught by the local judge. When a senior s. 96 judge came along to conduct a trial they were nice and polite to him, but they just did their business the way they always had, at the insistence of the local judge, knowing that the senior judge would be gone in a week — even faster if the case list collapsed, which they could usually arrange. So there was an ad hoc bureaucracy at the top level that was really designed and managed by the county judges. There was nothing wrong with that, but as we moved to professionalize the court staff and make them public service appointments, the court system was bound to change. There would be, as there is almost everywhere else in the world, a bureaucracy, a government bureaucracy that would run the court system. The question became and remains, to what extent should that bureaucracy be under the control of the public service and the taxpayers, and to what extent should it be controlled by the judges? There was much debate and as usual the Minister lost again. S. 78 of the Courts of Justice Act is the evidence of my defeat and spells out in a rough way the relationship between the judiciary and the court staff.

The last issue that I am able to identify in the process had to do with the design and management of judicial budgets. This remains a problem that has not been satisfactorily resolved and is not likely to be satisfactorily resolved in the present or any imaginable succeeding economic climate. The high water mark, from the judicial independence point of view of course, is part three of Chief Justice Deschene's report which contemplates a system in which the judges will deliver up a budget to the taxpayers' representatives and will, I take it, provoke a certain amount of debate, but I hope not interminable, before the allocation is passed. The proposal contained in the report has been the subject of prolonged debate and, while it is being debated, we are left with the present rather unsatisfactory system in which the Ministry of the Attorney General, as agent for the judicial system, goes to Treasury Board or Management Board to seek an allocation, which is then voted on by the legislature and is almost invariably judged, no doubt correctly, to be inadequate.

So this fourth issue in the interaction has to do with the management of court resources. All those issues are in flux and as we move forward, as we inevitably will over the next decade, to continued structural change we are going to have to address those four issues, and perhaps others which are clearly, even with respect to my narrow definition, very closely connected with the valued and important concept of judicial independence. Now I pray to God that Professor Lederman, whom I admired enormously, will not have found anything offensive in what I have said so far. He often did, but I hope he doesn't today.

NOTE

1. The text of this paper was prepared from the symposium transcript. Due to unfortunate circumstances, Mr. Scott was unable to review or edit the prepared text.

Methods of Appointment and Pluralism

Madam Justice Bertha Wilson[1]

Since the enactment of the Canadian *Charter of Rights and Freedoms* in 1982, conferring as it did substantially new powers on the judiciary and especially on the Supreme Court of Canada, public interest in the private personae of judges has escalated considerably. Canadians have been caught up in the high drama of Senate hearings in the United States and have been prompted to question the lack of scrutiny of candidates for the bench in our judicial appointment process. Newspaper and magazine articles trumpet headlines such as "Who judges the judges?" and there are increasing demands for interviews of judges and analyses of their personal philosophies. It is only the deeply ingrained traditional reticence of our Canadian judges to be exposed to the public shorn of their robes of office that has so far constrained the media.

John Brigham, a professor of political science at the University of Massachusetts, has described the situation in the United States in his book "The Cult of the Court"[2]. He points out that "the cult of the court" or "the cult of the judge" has replaced in modern times the traditional "cult of the robe". Traditionally, when judges donned their robes of office their private personae became submerged in the institution they served. The only thing that mattered in the administration of justice was their institutional personae. The judge was the high priest of justice with a special talent for elucidating the law. Professor Brigham states that judges in the United States are now emerging from their robes of office and becoming identified more and more as political actors.

It is not surprising therefore that Canadians are asking: Who are these people making fundamental decisions that affect our daily lives? Where did they come from and who placed them in these positions of power?

Professor Peter Russell, in an article entitled "Modernizing the Supreme Court"[3], says that the Court was a very second-rate institution until 1949, when appeals to the Privy Council were abolished. He says that at that point it started to improve, but very slowly. He attributes its slow progress to the government's tendency to make judicial appointments on the basis of party political affiliation rather than on the basis of merit.

Professor Lederman, in his article "Current Proposals for Reform of the Supreme Court of Canada"[4] expressed the same concern over the method of judicial appointments, stating that "loyalty to the political party in power is given priority over merit pure and simple". Quoting from the Canadian Bar Association Report of the Committee on the Constitution, entitled "Towards a New Canada", he states that we should be seeking "for the Court, the best and most sensitive judicial minds the nation has to offer".

The question is: How do you go about doing this? I don't think any right-minded person today would disagree with the objective. Indeed, it was reiterated time and time again in briefs presented to the Canadian Bar Association's Task Force on Gender Equality in the Legal Profession which I had the privilege to chair. However, the main thrust of these briefs was that women, and more particularly women belonging to Canada's minority groups, were seriously under-represented on Canada's judiciary. It was urged upon us that the existing appointment process was clearly, from the statistics, failing to reflect the twin principles of equality and diversity.

In discussing this issue with some of those involved in the appointing process and with judges, I was frequently told that appointing on the basis of equality and diversity was incompatible with appointing on the basis of merit, the assumption presumably being that if equality and diversity were ignored in the appointing process, as seems to be the case at present, the result would inevitably be appointments on merit. We would simply be derogating from the principle of merit by the principles of equality and diversity instead of, as previously, by the principle of party political affiliation. We would be no closer to the ideal of appointments based, as Professor Lederman put it, on "merit pure and simple".

It seems to me that the answer to this dilemma must lie in the meaning of "merit" in this context. Is there, in other words, such a thing as "merit pure and simple"? In order to answer that question we have to first ask ourselves: What qualities should we be looking for in a judge? It surprises me that many Canadian writers, who have critically reviewed the current appointing process and in many cases found it wanting, have been able to do so without forming some opinion, or at least articulating some opinion, as to the profile of "the good judge". How can you decide what process will produce good judges unless you know what you are looking for? We know, of course, that candidates must have certain professional qualifications, a number of years experience at the Bar, a good general knowledge of the law, no criminal record, an ability to maintain their independence from government and a degree of impartiality and objectivity in their approach to litigious issues. It is also helpful if they have good powers of legal analysis, an understanding of the decision-making process, and some writing skills. But what about their personal characteristics? What about things like intellectual humility, patience and an ability to listen, flexibility, moral courage, compassion for human frailty, respect for the human dignity of all persons regardless of their circumstances, and good sound common sense? Do you include these in the mix and, if you do, by what process do you decide whether or not the candidate has them or to what degree?

I believe that the public expects to find these qualities in their judges. I think they also expect their judges to be representative of the diversity of Canadian society. Yet we know that women and members of Canada's visible minorities are seriously under-represented on every court in the country, both in terms of the proportion of women and visible minorities in the general population and in terms of their proportion in the legal profession. It is not surprising therefore that the public is asking whether the existing appointing processes are meeting the twin principles of merit and representativeness.

I believe that we must broaden our concept of merit. I don't think it is either "pure" or "simple" if by "pure" we mean that all appointees must meet the same criteria and if by "simple" we mean to suggest that it is easy to measure one set of qualities against another. I think that we use merit in two different senses, the merit of the candidate in the sense that he or she has all or most of the qualities we think a judge should have, and the merit of the appointment in the sense that the appointment of this particular candidate meets a real need on the court. We must, in other words, look at the complement of judges on a court to make sure that we have a good "mix" as well as looking at the qualities and abilities of each individual member. It may be that to some extent this is happening already. I can recall, for example, when I was on the Ontario Court of Appeal, a quite prevalent view that appointments to that Court should alternate between judges elevated from the trial division and candidates appointed directly from the profession or from the academic community. It was assumed that this process would produce a strong court, drawing the best and brightest from all three constituencies. I understand that in Ontario today special efforts are made at the provincial court level to seek out female candidates and candidates from visible minorities. This does not mean that these candidates are not appointed on merit in the sense of their individual qualifications and personal characteristics. It means, in all likelihood, that the appointments are also meritorious because they fill a real need on the court. I think this is an important distinction that has to be made, whether we are appointing a candidate from one of Canada's minorities or a candidate with special expertise in criminal law. We need, in my opinion, make no apology for this, but we should apologize for the secrecy, mystery and hidden agenda with which we have shrouded the process. Why don't we articulate and publish the relevant criteria?

Why don't we make it clear to the public that this is not an easy exercise, and that a variety of considerations enter into it that have to do, not only with the qualifications and qualities of the candidate, but also with the needs of the court?

I would like to think that governments, perceiving the growing concern of the public over the increased powers of the judiciary, would seize the opportunity to review their appointing processes, amend them where necessary, and publish a full description of the various steps, the people involved, and the relevant criteria. I think this is subsumed under the general heading of the public's right to know. I think it would also go a long way towards restoring public confidence in the system.

I would like to say in closing that I don't want to see the process for federal judicial appointments in the United States introduced into Canada. Indeed, I think that, in light of recent experiences with Senate confirmation hearings, Americans are having second thoughts themselves about the public interrogation of candidates on policy questions, that may later come before them on the Bench. Sandra Day O'Connor, as I recall, was interrogated at great length about her views on abortion before the Senate confirmed her to the Supreme Court of the United States and one has to wonder what impact this had on the public's perception of her judicial objectivity on this issue. It seems totally out of keeping with our traditions to have candidates for the Bench publicly declare themselves on controversial policy issues in order to get themselves appointed. The American Bar Association roundly condemned the Republican Party for having a plank in its platform pledging to:

> work for the appointment of judges at all levels of the judiciary who respect traditional family values and the sanctity of innocent human life.

I am totally supportive of the public's right to know but I don't think it goes that far!

NOTES

1. Madam Justice Wilson was unable to attend the symposium. Her paper was read at the ymposium by Professor Beverley Baines of Queen's University.
2. John Brigham, *The Cult of the Court*, Philadelphia:Temple University Press, 1987.
3. Peter Russell, "Modernizing the Supreme Court", in Beaudoin, Gérald A., ed., *The Supreme Court of Canada*, Cowansville, Que: Les Editions YvanBlais, 1985.
4. (1979), 57 Can Bar Rev 688.

Judicial Independence and Justice: The Pillars and the Temple

An essay in honour of William Ralph Lederman, Q.C.
on the occasion of a Symposium in his honour,
Queen's University, October 22-23, 1993

Tom Cromwell

I.

One cannot speak about judicial independence in Canada without referring to the work of William Ralph Lederman. His 1956 Canadian Bar Review article[1] continues to be the *locus classicus*, a remarkable matching of a vitally important subject with a scholar of depth and vision. From the perspective provided by the passage of nearly forty years, it is safe to say that the importance of the subject and of Professor Lederman's contribution to it are only going to increase in the foreseeable future.

Judicial independence is at the centre of an array of issues about how Canadian society will be governed. At the operational end of this array, there are issues such as the judicial appointment process, the reform of the courts' institutional structures, judicial discipline and judicial administration. As Professor Lederman recognized, the subject of judicial independence is closer to the heart of our society than any one of these operational issues. At the conceptual end of the array, we recognize that judicial independence is ultimately concerned with society's commitment to the rule of law and impartial justice.

In this brief paper, I propose to reiterate very summarily what Professor Lederman identified as the key elements of judicial independence — the core of the arrangements essential to qualify a judiciary as independent. I then refer to the societal purposes served by these arrangements and link them to some of the current operational issues.

II.

Professor Lederman developed what he referred to as the *Act of Settlement* model for the Superior Courts which was the basis of his description of judicial independence. He summarized the key elements of this *Act of Settlement* model as follows:

(i)   The essential autonomy of the judges: Judges "have guaranteed tenure in office with assured public salaries and pensions. They cannot be instructed how to decide cases that come before them."[2]

This aspect of the *Act of Settlement* model is reflected in the arrangements in our Constitution for the Superior Courts. Sections 96, 99 and 100 set out what the Lord Atkin referred to as the "three principal pillars in the temple of justice".[3] These, of course, are appointment by the Governor General, security of tenure and security of salary.

(ii)   Judges are legally trained. The second element of the *Act of Settlement* model is that Superior Court Judges are appointed from among the Bar — a feature constitutionalized in s. 96 of the *Constitution Act 1867*.

(iii) The Superior Courts have plenary original jurisdiction in at least some important subjects. Professor Lederman attached great importance to the plenary original jurisdiction and general supervisory power over inferior tribunals, through judicial review. He also argued, and his position was in the end adopted by the courts, that there is a core of Superior Court jurisdiction which cannot be taken away by provincial legislation.[4]

(iv)   The courts adhere to fair procedure. Professor Lederman argued that the last element of the *Act of the Settlement* model was that the courts acted with several well known elements of procedural fairness.[5]

Professor Lederman also identified the institutional context which in his view justified and prhaps required courts of the *Settlement* model. In England and in Canada, the rule of law requires "impartial and disinterested umpires".[6] This is all the more true in Canada's federal system, where these umpires must provide authoritative interpretations of the division of legislative powers between the federal government and the provinces. As he put it:

Both directly and indirectly the Superior Courts promote impartial and objective application of laws to the persons and circumstance those laws contemplate by their terms, and it is important to remember that this includes the distributions and divisions of governmental powers ... effected by Constitutional Laws.[7]

The coming into force of the *Charter* strengthened this element of the argument, as well as adding a constitutional requirement for an independent and impartial tribunal for the trial of criminal cases.[8] As Chief Justice Dickson put it in a passage with which Professor Lederman concurred:

> ... the enactment of the Canadian *Charter of Rights and Freedoms* ... conferred on the courts another truly classic role: the defence of basic individual liberties and human rights against intrusions by all levels and branches of government. Once again, in order to play this deeply constitutional role, judicial independence is essential.[9]

Professor Lederman thus identified the need for disinterested and impartial umpires for civil, criminal and constitutional disputes as supporting and justifying an independent judiciary. The importance of impartiality is reinforced by the use of the words "independent and impartial" in s. 11(d) of the *Charter*, and has figured prominently in the jurisprudence. For example in *Valente v. The Queen*,[10] LeDain, J. for the Court, said:

> Both independence and impartiality are fundamental not only to the capacity to do justice in a particular case but also to individual and public confidence in the administration of justice. Without that confidence the system cannot command the respect and acceptance that are essential to its effective operation. It is, therefore, important that a tribunal should be perceived as independent, as well as impartial, and that the test for independence should include that perception. The perception of whether the tribunal enjoys the essential objective conditions or guarantees of judicial independence, and not a perception of how it will in fact act, regardless of whether it enjoys such conditions or guarantees.

Further, as Gonthier J. said in *R. v. Lippe*:

> As judicial independence is a safeguard for judicial impartiality, understanding of its full scope is important to the fullness of protection of judicial impartiality. This is particularly so as breaches of independence are generally more easily identifiable to factual circumstances and hence easier to prove than bias itself which is essentially a state of mind.[11]

To much the same effect, Chief Justice Lamer said in the same case:

> The overall objective of guaranteeing judicial independence is to ensure a reasonable perception of impartiality; judicial independence is but a "means" to this "end". If judges could be perceived as "impartial" without judicial "independence", the

requirement of independence would be unnecessary. However, judicial independence is critical to the public's perception of impartiality. Independence is the cornerstone, a necessary prerequisite for judicial impartiality.[12]

I conclude this section with two observations. First, the most important aspect of courts following the *Act of Settlement* model is that they must be presided by *impartial* judges. Second, the institutional arrangements consistent with judicial independence provide necessary, but of course, not sufficient conditions for such impartiality *to exist and to be seen to exist.*

III.

In this section, we move from the institutional conditions for an independent judiciary — Lord Atkin's "pillars" — and into the "temple of justice" itself. My point here is simple, but I submit, important. The main reason for maintaining an independent judiciary, that is, the need for decision-makers who are, and are seen to be impartial, is also the essential aspect tending to preserve such independence.

The first half of the point has already been made. At the base of the institutional arrangements for judicial independence is the preservation of the conditions of impartiality. The second half of the point, that such impartiality is the true guarantee of judicial independence, is the aspect I develop here.

The courts and the judiciary, like all of the enduring institutions of society, require for survival the confidence of the society they serve. As the Canadian Bar Association's Court Reform Task Force put it:

> Nothing is more important to public order and the legitimacy of government than public confidence in the independence, impartiality and justice of the courts. The existence of public confidence is essential for the effective operation of the courts, and its preservation and enhancement is their most important responsibility.[13]

The basic point, simply put, is that independence provides the conditions for impartiality, but that public confidence in judicial impartiality is what ultimately safeguards judicial independence. Alexander Hamilton recognized this when he pointed out that "the judiciary has neither influence over sword nor purse — neither force nor will but only judgment."[14] It is the long-term public confidence in the impartiality and, ultimately, the justice of these judgments that justifies endowing the judiciary with the conditions of independence and also provides the most fundamental guarantee of that independence.

Sir Ninian Stephen put the latter aspect most eloquently:

> What ultimately protects the independence of the judiciary is a community consensus that that independence is a quality worth protecting, the citizen being better

served if the judiciary is preserved from domination by those more overtly powerful elements of governments, on whose support the judiciary is dependent, yet whose exercise of power the judiciary is charged with keeping within bounds prescribed by law.[15]

Several points need to be made about this public confidence which is both the justification for and the ultimate guarantee of judicial independence. Public confidence, in this setting, must be distinguished from popularity. Confidence must be assessed over the long-term; it is the sum of reactions to thousands upon thousands of judgments rendered over time. It is highly influenced by tradition, by the enduring ideas (and ideals) of society. Confidence can be compared to that building up of layers of rock that we see everywhere in the limestone formations around Kingston. It is deeper, broader and less event-specific than popularity, but nonetheless susceptible to accretion and erosion.

The means by which confidence is maintained with respect to the judiciary are more subtle than with respect to the other branches of government. There is no election, vote on a motion or question period; the traditional understanding of judicial independence precludes these with respect to the judiciary. There are only very limited ways open to the judiciary to duck a controversial question and a long tradition that judges defend their decisions only once — in the reasons for decision. The primary vehicle for maintaining and enhancing confidence is ultimately the belief in the value of the rule of law, "... the belief that the major influence in judicial decisions is not *fiat* but principles which bind the judges as well as the litigants and which apply consistently ... today, and also yesterday and tomorrow."[16]

Confidence in the judicial branch is also an important contributor to confidence in *the other* branches of government. The courts stand between the powers of the state and the individual, most vividly in criminal matters but equally importantly in many others. This judicial check on executive and legislative power provides reassurance that the coercive powers of the state are subject to lawful authority, impartially assessed.

Finally, confidence is a product of both *reality* and *perception*. As justice must be done and manifestly be seen to be done, so confidence is enhanced or eroded by what is done and what is perceived. Our first Prime Minister understood this point, although somewhat cynically, as he described the judicial performance of Justices Taschereau and Fournier during the first session of the Supreme Court:

Neither of them opened their mouths from first to last but both *looked* very wise which possibly had the same effect on the audience as if they were wise.[17]

So to conclude this section, the key points are these. Judicial *independence* provides the necessary, although not sufficient conditions for judicial *impartiality*.

This is true with respect to both *actual* and *perceived* impartiality. Impartiality, both actual and perceived, is essential to maintain public confidence in the judiciary. Such public confidence is, in turn, essential to the preservation of the rule of law. It is also the fundamental guarantee of judicial independence.

IV.

Professor Lederman argued that judicial independence is a governmental good in its own right.[18] To support his point today, one must make clear some assumptions that I imagine were unquestioned in 1956. Prime among them is that a state premised on the rule of law is something worth preserving. This idea, in today's legal culture, is far from uncontroversial. Why is it, critics ask, that the appeal to principles, impartially and dispassionately analyzed, so often leads to the preservation of the existing order of power and privilege? How can there be anything in the order of impartiality when all human beings (judges, by gracious concession, not excluded) are the products of their background and experience? Why should these "un-responsible", "unaccountable judges" be given a significant role to play in the governance of a democratic society?

These are all, of course, legitimate questions, but they are probably not ones that can be addressed in a discussion of judicial independence. As Professor Lederman made clear, the idea of an independent judiciary is premised on a societal commitment to the rule of law. If that commitment is misplaced, the debate must take place at a more fundamental level. Judicial independence is a corollary of the deeper principle and, I think, cannot be discussed very meaningfully absent some allegiance to that deeper principle.

This point is not nearly so trivial as it may first appear. Both in the literature and in daily life, the extent of society's commitment to the rule of law is in contention. In scholarly literature, some contend that the courts are simply irrelevant; they have lost any effective say about how citizens interact on a day to day basis.[19] At the other end of the spectrum, some commentators argue that judges have lost their legitimacy because they no longer apply neutral (legal) principles but instead meddle in the social fabric by imposing their own views of justice on a baffled and ungrateful population.[20] In the popular press, some writers decry the courts' lack of commitment to human rights evidenced by "conservative" interpretations of, for example, discrimination on the basis of marital status. At the same time, other commentators ridicule the courts for being activist in protecting freedom of speech or the rights of an accused to a fair trial. In short, the extremes on both sides question the idea of the rule of law.

The same can be applied to judicial impartiality. At one extreme we are presented with the image of the judge as one untouched by worldly influence or sentiment; at the other, as one hopelessly biased by his or her upbringing and experience. Once again, there is not much use of speaking about judicial independence in absence of some commitment to judicial impartiality, however, broadly or narrowly that may be defined. Professor Lederman, by the way, was no dreamer on this score. He thought that the conditions of independence would stimulate persons of moral integrity to do their best — "[g]iven learning and ability as well as conscience, this will be a very effective best".[21] This is a modest, but realistic working definition of impartiality; without a belief in the value of impartial decisionmakers, there is not much point in talking about judicial independence. There is, of course, lots of middle ground and lots of grey area for reasoned argument. At a certain point, questioning the idea of judicial independence is really questioning the idea of the rule of law and the associated idea of impartial justice. Nothing is to be gained by masking it as anything else.

V.

Professor Lederman recognized the centrality of judicial independence to the larger questions of how we are governed. He placed the development of judicial independence in the context of major political developments in England and in Canada, concluding, for example, that recognition and strengthening of judicial independence accompanied great constitutional settlements.[22] He was also alive to some of the key "operational issues" to which judicial independence relates. In his 1956 article, he articulated some of the basic features of English Superior Courts and considered these central to his analysis of judicial independence. He returned to this theme in 1987, writing about Judicial Independence and Court Reform. He acknowledged the important link between judicial independence and the appointment process. You will recall that the concluding section of his 1956 article is devoted to the question of the appointment of judges. Professor Lederman not only saw judicial independence as a key element of political theory; he recognized some of the important day to day operational issues with which it is linked.

Court reform and judicial appointments, of course, do not exhaust the list of operational issues which implicate judicial independence. A good deal of literature in recent years has identified and discussed a wide range of such issues.[23] In the interest of time and space, I will simply list some of these issues with little elaboration:

- Judicial Appointments: The large measure of independence afforded judges is both justified and safeguarded by public confidence that the best available persons are appointed to the judiciary.

- Judicial Education: There have been calls for mandatory judicial education, particularly with respect to issues of systemic discrimination, gender bias and crosscultural awareness.

- Judicial Performance Evaluation: There have been calls for regular reviews of the judicial performance of judges.

- Judicial Discipline: A number of ideas are current in this area, including increased lay participation, more openness in the complaints process and a wider array of "sanctions" when misconduct is found to have occurred.

- Judicial Administration: There have been calls for increased judicial control of the courts' administration and budget.

- The Role of Chief Justices: Judicial independence is not only relevant at the institutional level, but at the individual level. It concerns not only the independence of the courts, but of each judge. There have been calls for some increased administrative authority for chief judges and administrative judges, but also some reservations expressed about the effect of such changes on the individual independence of the judges of the court.

This very quick summary demonstrates the almost bewildering array of current issues in which judicial independence, to some extent at least, is implicated. It is not my purpose to try to respond to each of these issues in detail; that would be beyond my mandate and the available space. What I will do is set out a few guiding principles that should be considered in tackling these and similar issues.

First, I submit that the starting point of all issues of judicial independence must be recognition of our commitment to the rule of law and the central place in it of impartial justice. There is lots of room to discern what we mean by "the rule of law" and "impartial justice", but absent some shared commitment to both, there is no point in talking about judicial independence.

Second, impartiality and independence must be assessed in fact and in perception.

Third, I suggest that the importance of public confidence in the judiciary be kept at the forefront of consideration. The special means by which this confidence is strengthened or eroded must be kept in mind.

Fourth, the special role of the judiciary to stand between the subject and the power of the Executive must always be considered. While executive incursion is not the only threat to judicial independence, it is the one to be most feared.

Fifth, judicial independence must be recognized as a core value: as Professor Lederman put it, a governmental good in its own right. We should not tinker with any of its fundamental aspects until there is a broad societal consensus that such change is necessary and desirable. It is, after all, one of our fundamental constitutional principles, one of our first things to be agreed upon and one of the last things we should be ready to change. I vividly remember Professor Lederman discussing constitutional amendment with us in our Advanced Constitutional Law Seminar in 1975-76. His advice was, characteristically, so profound that it at first appeared simplistic. He said that "when the game is not going well, the last thing to do is change the rules". He did *not* say that we should never change the rules, simply that we should be *slow* to change our *most fundamental rules*.

VI.

I recently heard on the radio a reading of some new poems by George Jonas. A couplet, which I can now only approximate, caught my attention:

> "A dreamer's ship wrecks on a fact,
> A prudent man's on a dream"

This is good advice for us as we deal in fundamental constitutional values such as judicial independence. We must be dreamers or idealists, insisting on the preservation of the great principles of our society even, no — especially, when convenience would point us towards doing otherwise. We must also be practical; our institutions have to work in current conditions and respond to the needs of today's people, not to those of the barons assembled at Runnymede. The key is balance, a balance that is refreshingly evident in Willam Ralph Lederman's scholarship on the subject of judicial independence, a balance that places us in his debt and which we would all do well to emulate.

NOTES

1. W.R. Lederman, "The Independence of the Judiciary", (1956) 34 Can. Bar Rev. 769-809; 1139-1179.
2. W.R. Lederman, "Judicial Independence and Court Reform in Canada for the 1990's", (1987), 12 *Queen's Law Journal* 385, at p. 389.
3. *Toronto v. York Twsp.*, [1938] 1 D.L.R. 593, at p. 594.
4. See Lederman, *op. cit.* note 1, at pp. 1166-1175.
5. These four elements are set out in Lederman, *op cit.*, note 2, at pp. 389-391.
6. *Ibid.*, at p. 397.
7. Lederman, *op. cit.*, note 1, at p. 1178.
8. Part I of the *Constitutional Act 1982*, s. 11(d).
9. *The Queen v. Beauregard* (1987), 30 D.L.R. (4th) 481 (S.C.C.) at p. 493.
10. [1985] 2 S.C.R. 673 at 689.
11. *R. v. Lippe*, [1991] 2 S.C.R., 114 at 156.
12. *Ibid.*, at 139.

13. Canadian Bar Association Court Reform Task Force, *Court Reform in Canada*, (1991), at pp. 46-47.

14. A. Hamilton, *The Federalist*, Chapter 78 (reference to be completed).

15. Sir Ninian M. Stephen, "Judicial Independence — A Fragile Bastion", in S. Shetreet and J. Deschenes (eds.) *Judicial Independence: The Contemporary Debate*, (1985) 529-545, at p. 534.

16. Archibald Cox, *The Warren Court*, (1968), 21-2; quoted in Stephen, *op. cit.*, note 15, at 534.

17. J.A. Macdonald, PAC. E. Blake Papers reel 241, no. 134 referred to in James G. Snell and Frederick Vaughan, *The Supreme Court of Canada, History of the Institution* (1985), at p. 25.

18. Lederman, *op. cit.*, note 1, at p. 1158.

19. See, for example, S.F.C. Milsom, "The Pact and Future of Judge — Made Law" (1981), 8 Monash Univ.L.Rev. 1 and G. Palmer, "The Growing Irrelevance of the Civil Courts" (1985) 5 Windsor Yrbk. Access to Justice 327.

20. Concern along these lines is expressed by Sir Ninian Stephen, see note 15; the more extreme version of the point is made by Eugene W. Hickok and Gary L.M. McDowell, *Courts and Politics in American Society* (1993).

21. Lederman, *op. cit.*, note 1, at p. 1178.

22. *Op. cit.*, note 1 at 1157.

23. A good overview of the issues found in James C. MacPherson, "Judging the Judges", unpublished speech prepared for a panel at the Annual Meeting of the Canadian Bar Association, Halifax, 1992.

AFTERWORD

Remembering Professor Lederman

George Thomson[1]

I'm very pleased to be here this evening and to be part of today's symposium and dinner in honour of Bill Lederman, or Dean Lederman as I always knew him. You'll be pleased to know that I don't propose to make what would be a very modest contribution to today's constitutional analysis and discussions, nor do I propose to list Bill's accomplishments as a scholar, teacher and Dean along with a very long list of honourary degrees and awards. Any one of those accomplishments — for example, in Patrick Monahan's words becoming the "most articulate creator and defender of modern constitutional theory" or being the first dean of a then struggling and now highly respected law school, or teaching more than 3,800 students in a long teaching career — more than justified the praise that we offered today. Taken together they are a remarkable catalogue of one person's abilities, interests and influence on his immediate community, on his profession and, in fact, on his country.

Now I knew Bill Lederman not only as my Dean and teacher but also as someone who gave me advice and guidance in key stages in my career. He will be remembered by all of the Thomson family as a family friend who sat a few pews away at St. Andrews Presbyterian Church. Tonight I would like to talk a bit about those parts of his life that I knew best, while passing on some memories from a number of his friends, family and colleagues, many of whom are here tonight.

Like a disproportionate number of Canada's leading scholars, jurists and public servants, he spent his early years in Saskatchewan, where wheat and service to the community seemed to be the two main crops. Both Brian Dickson and Sandy McPherson, his classmates, say that Bill acquired early his passion for writing and his determination to understand clearly any subject he took on. It was in high school that he first established his customary practice of always obtaining the highest grades.

Without romanticizing the terrible costs of the Depression and the War, it is possible to acknowledge that it shaped the core of some people's character in a way that nothing else might have. I've been told that in Bill's case it may have produced his sense of resolve, patience and endurance, his ability to make a commitment to friends and to live up to that commitment, his modesty and his gentleness of spirit. I assume these events also reinforced his early support for a strong central government and provided a grounding for his later conviction that constitutional analysis is inadequate without an understanding of context.

Service in the armed forces in World War II required Rhodes Scholars of the late 30's and early 40's to delay their studies at Oxford, which is why a small contingent of very bright Canadians including Bill Lederman, Doug Cameron, Bert McKinnon and Gordon Blair found themselves learning together after the war and forming friendships that lasted a lifetime.

When I arrived at Queen's law school as one of Bill's 3,800 students, he had been dean for four years. The small number of students, less than 100 in the whole school, a narrow and more fixed curriculum, the less complex external economic and social environment, the homogeneity of the student body, were all factors that made his role as dean different than it would be today. However, this doesn't alter the fact that there was something special about the law school over which Dean Lederman presided. It was tied very much to the personality and the style of our dean and the small number of members of faculty. Now it's a sure sign of aging when one puts a nostalgic gloss on the past, but I can think of several examples of that unique environment such as the 25 minute break each day between the 2nd and 3rd class so that we could drink coffee and play cribbage together, and the special relationship with the faculty who were our friends and who attended all our social gatherings. In fact the problem wasn't getting them to the social gatherings, it was getting them to go home afterwards.

The Ledermans gave small dinners in their home week after week each academic year until they had covered the entire student body. I remember my group driving home talking about how amazing it was that our taciturn dean had such an effervescent and outgoing spouse. As a student, I found him quiet and shy but also friendly and accessible. Bill cared deeply for his wife and children. It must have been a source of great pride when he ended up with not two but four lawyers in the family, and when Bill jr. decided to enter the ministry.

Our dean was firm when a crises hit, such as the new professor who spent two months explaining and re-explaining one complex company law case to us until the dean stepped in and put him out of his misery. He unfailingly treated us as adults, although I don't remember giving him much reason to do so. We spent enormous amounts of time trying to decipher what have since become known as "the sayings of Chairman Bill," including "it's a long alley with no overturned ash cans," "life is too short for instant coffee," and "there's no point having a dog if you have to bark for it."

Bill Lederman possessed most, if not all, of those characteristics that seemed essential to survival as a dean, then and now, such as a belief in democratic decision making coupled with an ability to do the extra work to ensure that democracy never ran amok; care taken never to overuse the powers of the office; a willingness to nurture relationships with the broader university community, coupled with an absolute insistence that the law school be supported by the University on key issues like faculty recruitment and support, the new building and, in particular, the need for a large, well stocked library. A major contributing factor to the school's and Bill's success was the strong personal and professional support he received from Principal Bill McIntosh and from another Saskatchewan native and fellow Rhodes Scholar, Alex Corry.

Bill was open to new ideas, at least after giving them the careful analysis only he could give them. The best example I know of was the decision to add nine student members to the faculty board at a time when other law schools viewed the prospect with alarm and when the students themselves were seeking only eight places at the table.

Now, as a totally honest former student I have to acknowledge that there were times in class, when an old Bob and Rae skit would come briefly to mind, the one involving an interview with the president of the "Slow Talkers of America Association". However, his classes were also welcomed as a respite from the frenetic and occasionally terrifying environments created by his more socratically oriented colleagues. Orderly, balanced lectures, combined with what Ian Scott has described as his ability to write and teach simply and plainly about great constitutional issues, meant we were always perfectly ready for exams. We were aided by the fact that he was so eager to see us do well that we always had a pretty good idea of what would be facing us in the exam room.

In Jurisprudence he went too far and gave us the six questions in advance. Given our team approach to preparation it meant that to this day my knowledge of jurisprudence is limited to a quite detailed understanding of the contributions of the American Realist school of jurisprudential analysis. In retrospect, I believe what he taught us most effectively was an appreciation of what's involved in knowing a subject well and for the level of scholarship required to fully analyze the complex issues he presented to us so carefully and clearly.

After I left law school, he never failed to write to me when I changed jobs and, to those who know me well, this meant I heard from him fairly often. He had a great respect for the judiciary and for those who took on government service. He worried, quite rightly it turns out, that I was leaving law teaching before achieving a firm grounding and an established level of scholarship in my field. Of course he told me so in the gentlest and most careful way possible.

Several friends with whom I have spoken have provided me with some examples which illustrate the characteristics that I was exposed to in law school. His quiet, self-effacing style meant that it took the combined persuasive efforts of Alex Corry and Gordon Blair to get him to see the value of pulling his remarkable and wide ranging essays together into one book. Modest about himself, he was eager to acknowledge the strong influence and support of others such as Cory, Robert MacGregor Dawson, Myrtle McPherson, his boyhood Saskatchewan friends, and his long time colleagues at Queen's. Many spoke of the Queen's law school as his second home and of the faculty and students as almost a second family. Edna Lederman gave me perhaps the best example of his reluctance to speak about himself. She remembered listening to him engage in a political discussion in Saskatchewan not long after they were married and then suddenly saying to herself "My God, I married a liberal."

He believed strongly that progress could be made on an issue if those involved treated each other with respect and fairness; this may help to explain his intense disappointment when he perceived others falling short of that standard, during his only appearance before the Supreme Court of Canada and again when he testified before a Senate Committee dealing with repatriation of the Constitution. For him, the ideal outside work involved careful research and providing advice to bodies such as the McRuer Commission on Civil Rights, the Ontario Advisory Committee on Confederation and the Law Reform Commission.

Bill was very careful not to do anything he thought might compromise his independence as a scholar, which explains why he very rarely took on work that might place him in an advocacy position on behalf of a particular client. I think he must have viewed with some disquiet those recent major media events called constitutional negotiations, where each government is surrounded by its appropriate share of strategists, advisors and advocates, academic and otherwise. It's also worth noting that he held to this approach notwithstanding the serious effect it probably had on his outside income and even though it meant that he fell into some disfavour when his independent perspectives called into question the constitutional plans of the federal government and its then prime minister.

As his former student and a Kingston friend, it seemed to me, of course, that Bill accomplished so much without ever straying from either the law school or his home on Johnson Street, where he and Edna lived for 34 years. I must say that I found some comfort in that belief, given that I can stand on the front steps of Macdonald Hall and see the front of the building in which I attended public school, high school, undergraduate arts and law school. Thus, it was a surprise to discover that, at various times, he taught at Saskatchewan, Dalhousie, Osgoode, Victoria, McGill, and the University of Montreal, not to mention his time at Oxford and the work he did to develop a constitution for the new government of Papua, New Guinea.

Bill was a keen student of Canadian history and his fascination with the political process goes back as far as the days when he, Brian Dickson and Sandy McPherson sat in the Speakers' Gallery in the Saskatchewan Legislature and listened to the debates. I think all of this helped in the development, over time, of his belief in the importance of regional diversity and respect for the values that oppose a central power that is too strong, and in the balancing exercise that gives weight to historical context and precedent but then goes on to ask deceptively simple questions such as, "Is it better for the people that this thing be done on a national level or on a provincial level"?

Two more observations about him. He developed his positions carefully and a quick look at his collection of essays shows that his stand on some issues changed over time, but he wasn't easily pushed or shaken once he made up his mind and he was very firm when the matter touched a basic value. For example, he took a firm stand when the university was slow to recognize the need for a convocation ceremony that did not emphasize one particular religious faith, or when it continued to use an application form that asked questions that might permit the making of unfair admissions decisions. Given his strong views on compulsory retirement, I assume it was good for their long friendship when Mr. Justice Blair dissented from the majority Court of Appeal decision that held that compulsory retirement laws are not unconstitutional.

Much will have been said today about his contribution to our understanding of constitutional law and the enormous range of issues that he dealt with in his work. I know well that in 1955 he wrote about how judicial independence might be affected by government decisions on salaries and court administration — a topic that a typical 1993 deputy attorney general working for a cash starved government spends enormous amounts of time debating and worrying about. I'll only make two observations about Bill's approach to constitutional law. The first is obvious but worth saying again, which is that when one knows who Bill Lederman was as a person, it becomes quite understandable that his major contribution was to help us understand that constitutional doctrine is always an expression of fundamental values and that constitutional analysis requires a careful balancing approach that examines the values that underlie each of the competing positions.

Equally understandable were Bill's recognition that the individual values of a judge play a role in the process, and his assertion that a decision cannot be made without a careful analysis of precedent and history, and an understanding of the social, economic and political context within which the matter is being considered.

I think that anyone who knew Bill Lederman as a churchman, friend, dean or teacher, would describe him in a way that liberally makes use of such words as balanced, careful, and adherent to fundamental values. As might be expected, the distinctions between the man and his scholarship seem very indistinct.

Finally, I would make one obvious point. Over the last year, I obtained what for the group called "constitutional experts" is seen to be an essential first badge of membership these days: I participated in a failed set of constitutional negotiations. As a result, I'm increasingly aware of how much our future may depend upon the existence of people like Bill Lederman who are able to find balanced solutions within a process that involves such diverse and competing interests.

NOTE

1.   Deputy Attorney General, Ontario

Selected Works of W.R. Lederman

BOOKS

Continuing Canadian Constitutional Dilemmas: Essays on the Constitutional History, Public Law and Federal System of Canada, (Toronto: Butterworths, 1981)

Canadian Constitutional Law: Cases, Notes and Materials (3d ed. with J.D. Whyte and D.F. Bur 1992; 2d ed. with J.D. Whyte 1977; 1st ed. with J.D. Whyte 1975 (Toronto: Butterworths)

The Courts and the Canadian Constitution: A Selection of Essays (ed.) (Toronto: McClelland & Stewart, 1964)

ARTICLES

"Judicial Independence and Court Reforms in Canada for the 1990's" (1987), 12 Queen's L. J. 385.

"Constitutional Procedure and Reform of the Supreme Court of Canada" (1985), 26 Cahiers de Droit 195

"Democratic Parliaments, Independent Courts and the Canadian Charter of Rights and Freedoms" (1985), 11 Queen's L. J. 1.

"Canadian Constitutional Amending Procedures: 1867-1982" (1984), 32 Am. J. Comp. Law 339

"The Canadian Charter of Rights and Freedoms: One Year Later" (1983), 21 Transactions of the Royal Society of Canada (Series IV).

Comment: "Supreme Court of Canada and Basic Constitutional Amendment: An Assessment of *Reference Re Amendment of the Constitution of Canada (Nos. 1, 2 and 3)* (1982), 27 McGill L. J. 527.

"The Power of the Judges and the New *Canadian Charter of Rights and Freedoms*" (1982), 16 U.B.C. Law Rev. 1.

Comment: "Amendment and Patriation" (1981), 19 Alta. L. Rev. 372.

"Mr. Justice Rand and Canada's Federal Constitution" (1980), 18 U. W. O. Law Rev. 31.

"Current Proposals for Reform of the Supreme Court of Canada" (1979), 57 Can. Bar Rev. 687.

"Constitutional Amendment and Canadian Unity" in *Special Lectures of the Law Society of Upper Canada* (Toronto: Richard de Boo, 1978) 17.

"Unity and Diversity in Canadian Federalism: Ideals and Methods of Moderation" (1975), 53 Can. Bar Rev. 597.

"Comparing the Constitutions of Canada and the United States" (1975), 61 Amer. Bar Assoc. Jour. 710

"The British Parliamentary System and Canadian Federalism" in R.M. Burns, ed., *One Country or Two?* (Montreal: McGill-Queen's Univ. Press, 1971) 17.

"Canadian Legal Education in the Second Half of the Twentieth Century" (1971), 21 U T. L. J. 141.

"Thoughts on Reform of the Supreme Court of Canada" (1970), 8 Alta. L. Rev. 1.

"Some Forms and Limitations of Co-operative Federalism" (1967), 45 Can. Bar Rev. 409.

"The Process of Constitutional Amendment for Canada" (1966), 12 McGill L. J.. 371.

"Law Schools and Legal Ethics" (1965), 8 Can. Bar J. 212.

"The Balanced Interpretation of the Federal Distribution of Legislative Powers in Canada" in P.A. Crépeau and C.B. MacPherson, eds., *The Future of Canadian Federalism* (Toronto: University of Toronto Press, 1965) 91.

"The Concurrent Operation of Federal and Provincial Laws in Canada" (1963), 9 McGill L. J. 185.

"The Nature and Problems of a Bill of Rights" (1959), 37 Can. Bar Rev. 769 and 1139.

"The Common Law System in Canada" in E. McWhinney, ed. *Canadian Jurisprudence: The Civil Law and Common Law in Canada* (Toronto: Carswell, 1958) 34.

"The Independence of the Judiciary" (1956), 34 Can. Bar Rev. 769 and 1139.

"Conflict Avoidance by International Agreement" (1956), 21 Law & Contem. Prob. 581.

"Classification of Laws and the British North America Act" in J.A. Corry, F.C. Cronkite, and E.F. Whitmore, eds., *Legal Essays in Honour of Arthur Moxon* (Toronto: University of Toronto Press, 1953) 183.

"Classification in Private International Law" (1953), 29 Can. Bar Rev. 3 and 168.